THE SEXUAL CHRISTIAN

THE SEXUAL CHRISTIAN

TIM STAFFORD

VICTOR BOOKS®

A DIVISION OF SCRIPTURE PRESS PUBLICATIONS INC.
USA CANADA ENGLAND

Recommended Dewey Decimal Classification: 241
Suggested Subject Heading: CHRISTIAN ETHICS

Library of Congress Catalog Card Number: 88-62849
ISBN: 0-89693-622-8

Cover Illustration: Tim Jonke

CONTENTS

ACKNOWLEDGMENTS

I want particularly to thank my brother, William Stafford, for sharing his insights and historical knowledge. He answered many questions and let me read some of his work in progress. I borrowed extensively. He also read my second chapter in manuscript form and made helpful suggestions.

Philip Yancey read the entire book in manuscript form, and was a great help and encouragement. Rodney Clapp, my editor for this project at *Christianity Today*, did the same. It is a joy to have such friends and colleagues.

Finally, I want to acknowledge the support and love of my wife, Popie, without whom this book would not be possible, in more ways than one.

Chapter 1

THE ETHIC OF INTIMACY

*H*i. *I am 18 years old. I need your help. My boyfriend and I are really serious. We're talking about marriage in a couple of years. We have made love more than once. It feels so right, but I know it's so wrong. See, I was brought up in a strong Christian family. I know I'm doing wrong in God's eyes. But it just feels so right when we're together. Just like it was meant to be. I don't feel guilty about making love with him. We both love each other so much. I keep telling myself I'll stop, but when we're together it all just feels so right."*

• *"I am only 18 years old, and I am petrified that I have AIDS. It is not that I live in New York or Chicago where AIDS runs rampant; in fact, where I live may not even be on the map! It is the fact that I have had eight sexual partners in the past year, from all backgrounds. I thought nothing of it at the time; I was just 'sowing wild oats,' blowing off steam, looking for something I wasn't supposed to have. I had never done those things (drinking, sex) before, and I don't now. There was just approximately a year in my life when I took leave of my senses and went literally wild. Now I'll be wondering about that year for perhaps fifteen more (I understand AIDS can stay dormant for that long)."*

• *"My boyfriend's dad talked to him last night and told him that he must have sex. His dad thinks it is a part of love and that he must be experienced before he gets married. I know his mom doesn't think the same, but his dad is the head of the house and also the strict authority over it. His dad told him if he didn't have sex, then we would have to break up."*

• *"I'm 17 years old and I'm still a virgin. No problem, right? Wrong! I feel like I am the only one, and I've been wondering why I'm even bothering to save my virginity for the man I marry when all the guys I know aren't virgins. I keep asking God to save me one, but I haven't met any."*

• *"In September of '84 I had my first steady girlfriend. I was a little on the shy side, while she was quite aggressive. She initiated all our sexual activity. I hardly knew her and I knew I didn't love her, but she was nice and attractive. We dated three months and then she decided she wanted to go out with other guys, so we broke up.*

"Should I tell my new girlfriend about it? We do nothing like that and we've been going out for two years. How do I get rid of the bad feelings I have inside?"

• *"I used to be a real churchgoer until I met a girl I really liked. I kept telling myself and God that the most that would happen would be that I would kiss the girl. Well, one thing led to another, and we ended up having sex. The first two or three times I felt really guilty and I repented and told God I would never do it again. Well, now we have sex and I don't feel guilty. But I feel that my separation from God is permanent."*

For the past 15 years I have written a sort of "Dear Abby" column for *Campus Life*, a Christian magazine for high school and college-age young people. You have just read a small sample of the many thousands of letters I have received from teenage kids all over America, letters scrawled semilegibly on lined paper ripped out of school notebooks, letters printed prettily on butterfly stationery, letters typed on white bond. These letters give one a feeling for received culture—how theory actually percolates down to the grass-roots. Margaret Mead's classic study, *Coming of Age in Samoa*, may not have precisely stated that promiscuity is a boon to society, but that was the message the average college freshman got. Similarly, there are messages about sex percolating down into our colleges and high schools and junior high schools today.

When I sit down with a bulging file folder of these letters, perhaps the most striking impression I get is one of confusion and of the pain that comes with this confusion. Sex has undoubtedly always mattered to teenagers, but kids today inhabit a society that constantly stimulates sexual desire (in movies, on TV, in music, even on billboards) and offers many opportunities for sex (particularly in bedrooms when parents are working or gone for the evening). As a result, more kids are sexually active than in years past, and they become sexually active younger. Inexperienced teenagers often feel ashamed of their virginity.

Few parents talk easily or regularly about sex to their children. If the kids are lucky, their parents give them the facts of life in a single formal session. Many parents are themselves confused, and they often convey a double message: I wish you'd wait to have sex, but I know you probably won't. Schools offer a detached, biological perspective on sex. And the church says little. On the whole, our society offers no sexual standards for the way kids are to behave. Its message is merely that old parental standard: "Be careful."

So kids write to me. Their letters range from the trivial ("There is this boy in geometry who I think I love. I always smile at him, but he never says anything to me. How do I know if this is really love?") to the tragic ("We made love often in the two years we were together. It really was 'making love.' But since she went away to college she says I am clinging to her. I honestly don't want to cling, but I think about her constantly. I write her these long letters. I have considered killing myself, though I know it wouldn't solve anything."). I answer these letters as best I can, trying to give practical advice but also some Christian perspective.

Fortunately, *Campus Life* lets me write answers much longer than Dear Abby's. But I am quite aware of my powerlessness. A magazine column cannot substitute for the solidarity and care that a community should offer. I can give advice and a little perspective, but I cannot give what they most need—another world to live in.

The need for a counterculture
The church ought to provide another world, a society that strengthens, encourages, teaches, and models a distinctive way of living

sexually. The church ought to be a sexual counterculture for these kids, yet it isn't.

True, most Christians still stand for a distinct set of standards—no sex outside of marriage, for example—but it is not clear from sociological studies whether Christians behave much differently from their worldly peers. Nor is it clear that they *think* differently in their basic expectations of what life and love and sex have to offer. If they do think differently, they are not doing a very good job of communicating it to their children.

It is our *thinking* about sex that I particularly want to consider in this book. Even though our society gives no clear guidance about what is sexually right and wrong, it does have a point of view. I will argue that its point of view contributes tremendously to the pain and confusion of people's lives. That in itself does not, from a Christian perspective, make it wrong. If pain and pleasure were the main criteria for sizing up a style of life, how would Christians justify their faith while living in, say, the Soviet Union?

To our pragmatic age, though, the test of pain and pleasure is crucial. So I will attempt, among other tasks, to judge our time by its own standards. Does our society's approach to sexuality work as advertised? All its claims are based on the promise that life will get better. Is the promise fulfilled?

I say our society has a sexual point of view, though some might disagree. Many voices vie with one another: feminists, Freudians, behaviorists, Jungians, Reichians, New Age thinkers, sociobiologists, sexual gourmets. But this mélange of voices, after it is strained through the media, does attain a certain degree of coherence. That is why I begin with letters from teenagers, and will often cite pop authorities, such as Dr. Ruth—for grassroots culture is what affects high school kids, as well as, I daresay, therapists, judges, legislators, school administrators, parents, and journalists. They operate on "common sense," on "what everybody knows."

I will try to articulate "what everybody knows," partly so that Christians can see how those thoughts have infiltrated their own minds. Then I will go on to describe a Christian view of sex—a view that contradicts not only our society's point of view, but some long-held Christian orthodoxies.

A short history lesson

It is a major preoccupation of culture—some would say *the* preoccupation of culture—to decide how to organize itself sexually. For the last fifteen hundred years, up until about 1950, Western culture (outside the monasteries) had a broad consensus on its sexual organization. Of course, the Old Consensus was often broken, and it did change with the times (when, for instance, marriages stopped being arranged by parents). But the taboos—incest, adultery, divorce—and the goal—lifelong, monogamous marriage—stayed reasonably stable.

The history of how this Old Consensus came into being is complicated, but suffice it to say that the New Testament was only one influence. Monogamy was already prevalent in first-century Judaism; the New Testament elevated it, preaching in the strongest terms against divorce, against adultery, against promiscuity, against prostitution, against any "safety valves" that Greco-Roman culture held to be harmless, even helpful, to the strength of the institution. The New Testament's monogamy is a pure monogamy.

And it is a loving monogamy—not merely a convenient social compact, but a covenant to be filled with love as a cup is filled with wine. Nowhere does the Bible say that love is the basis for marriage; but it does claim that marriage is the basis for love. Paul's command is "Husbands, love your wives," rather than "Men, marry your lovers." Within marriage one is to love—within the covenant set up between not merely individuals, but families, and enforced by the church and the community. Marriage is easily defined in legal terms. It has a beginning that can be dated precisely. It is an institution, while love is not. Ideally, the two should be congruent, but the institution is the starting point in the New Testament. The cup is necessary before the wine can be poured.

The pure monogamy of the New Testament was soon adulterated. Western society added several unbiblical elements to its framework. One is the double standard. A man who broke the rules was often winked at, but a woman rule breaker was ostracized. Prostitution was generally tolerated; even theologians as rigorous as Augustine or Aquinas were at a loss to imagine how a stable society could operate without "a sewer," as Aquinas referred to it. "Take away the sewer and you will fill the palace with pollution. . . . Take away prostitutes from the world and you will fill it with sodomy." Most medieval cities in Christian Europe had well-organized, thoroughly accepted streets of prostitution.

Also added was a degraded view of sex, as belonging to humanity's lower nature. The Bible, for all its strictness about sex, takes a profoundly positive view of it, as part of creation; but the church, perhaps influenced by Stoic philosophy, came to think that its spiritual leaders should all be celibate. Sex was treated as a danger. Augustine concluded that original sin itself was passed on through sex. Though the Reformation brought marriage back into honor, the belief that sex was from our dark side persisted. Sexual desire was to be hushed up, repressed, risen above.

Between 1945 and 1965 this Old Consensus, after centuries of stability, broke up. The sexual revolution had been taking shape for decades, even centuries, and some of its presuppositions had gained acceptance long before. However, most people's expectations remained conventional: First comes love, then comes marriage, then comes Mary with a baby carriage.

Then, suddenly, sexual freedom broke out of the province of freethinking intellectuals and artists, and very quickly became the common person's view. This was triggered not by an intellectual breakthrough, but by two medical breakthroughs: penicillin and the Pill. The first could cure syphilis, which is a highly contagious, deadly disease. Sleeping around no longer meant risking your life. The second prevented babies far more efficiently than previous methods of birth control, and thus suggested that sex's connection to family was unnecessary. Sex could be, for the first time in history, separated from life-and-death consequences. Understandably, people's views of sex became more liberal, and so did their behavior.

The Playboy experiment: Rejected
Since America has recently grown more conservative, some may hope that the Old Consensus is returning. They would be mistaken. Sexually, the swing back toward the Old Consensus has been extremely modest, if perceptible at all. What has happened is that the Playboy experiment has been rejected.

The sexual revolution spurred a variety of views on sex, and the Playboy experiment was only one. Hugh Hefner probably did the most to convey it to the masses, but others said essentially the same thing with more sophistication. They often referred to Sigmund Freud and his theories about sexual repression, but their real intellectual ancestor was Jean Jacques Rousseau, who thought that humanity in the wild state was naturally good and happy, but was spoiled by society. That such dreaming should endure for two centuries is remarkable, for to this day, no happy humanity unspoiled by society has been found. (An occasional "wild child" is found in the forest, but it has proven difficult to call such a child's inarticulate, animalistic behavior happy and good.) Men and women inevitably live in society, and societies always have ways of organizing their sexual behavior. Yet, still one can hear speculations about, for instance, how many people would be homosexually oriented if society had no influence on them; or whether humankind is naturally monogamous. Humankind is not naturally anything, if by "natural" we mean without social imperatives.

The Playboy experiment, however, blamed much unhappiness on sexual repression. It urged people to act on their blessedly natural sexual urges. A good number of people tried life by this ethic, and some are still trying it. But we can now consider the experiment rejected. It did not lead to the disastrous disruption of society that some moralists predicted. (At least, it has not yet. But then, we have not yet seen the full impact of its medical consequences, let alone its social consequences.) Long before any full-scale disaster broke out, people began losing interest in the Playboy philosophy. They discovered that they wanted love more than sex. "How to have a good relationship," not "How to have good sex," is at the editorial foundation of most general-interest publications today.

What made the Playboy experiment a failure for most people was not AIDS or other sexually transmitted diseases, but loneliness. Masters and Johnson chipped in by pointing out that sexual pleasure was highest in a caring relationship. A new ethic began to evolve: the Ethic of Intimacy.

Traditionalists may have a hard time seeing how the Ethic of Intimacy is different from the Playboy experiment; under both, most people expect to pair up with a number of partners during their lifetime. Some time ago I was having lunch with two older pastors, and when I told them I was writing about modern sexual ethics, they shook their heads, smiled, and said they didn't realize there were any. To them, any ethic but the Old Consensus is a non-ethic.

But the Ethic of Intimacy is quite distinct from the Playboy experiment. For one, it is moderately positive about marriage. You don't see so much written now about the crippling inhibitions society imposes; the Old Consensus is no longer an enemy so much as an unrecoverable past. Sexual freedom is a given in the new ethic, but it is not an end. It is to be guided by the ideal of intimacy.

Intimacy is not love, exactly. It is a state two people may feel for a night, or a month, or a lifetime. Though women's magazines contain a good deal of advice on it, intimacy is a quality we cannot precisely describe. Most people would say, I think, that you know it when you feel it. The Ethic of Intimacy offers no behavioral absolutes, but many attitudinal absolutes, such as openness and caring. It is these attitudes, and the personal feelings between two people, that make up intimacy.

The Old Consensus did have behavioral absolutes, for its linchpin was marriage. You could define right and wrong as precisely as you could define the institution. Today the demarcations are blurry, either coming in or going out of relationship. Couples are expected first to sleep together, then live together in a kind of trial marriage, then finally (if things work out), to ratify their state in a ceremony. People still take vows, though what they are vowing and why is unclear. Going out of relationship, divorced and widowed people are now included as "singles"; they are lumped with people who have never been married, as though marriage had made no difference. Ultimately, people are categorized as "currently attached" or "available." That is why some women's magazines do not use the terms "husband" and "wife" much any more. The current terms are generic: "partner" or "lover." This is not antimarriage. It is mildly positive about marriage. But marriage does not come first. Intimacy does.

Actually, the Ethic of Intimacy has been developing for centuries. One might even blame it on the early church, which insisted that since marriage was to be loving, both husband and wife must assent to their marriage. (This was scandalous advice to many parents, who had no intention of asking their children's advice on a good marriage.) Much later, near the end of the seventeenth century, children began to choose their own partners, and *parents*, rather than children, were left with veto power. By our own time (in Western culture), parents had no say at all. Sheer romantic love was viewed as the only proper justification for marriage. As a smitten girl in Rodgers and Hammerstein's *Carousel* put it: "What's the use of wondering if he's good or if he's bad? . . . He's your feller and you love him. That's all there is to that." A great many people who supported the Old Consensus accepted that line and even sentimentally wept over it. But in doing so, they were undermining the Old Consensus.

The Ethic of Intimacy takes Rodgers and Hammerstein just one step further. If a person's character means nothing in the face of love, then surely the niceties of a marriage ceremony mean even less. What matters is simply the particular feelings inspired when two people are together. Everything depends on that magical spark of intimacy—its presence or its absence.

Seven features of the Ethic of Intimacy

In order to understand the way people apply the Ethic of Intimacy, we need a more detailed understanding. They do more than surrender to their feelings. They do so within a particular set of assumptions, so fundamental that they are rarely articulated.

1. *An invariably positive view of sex.* Any threads of the old belief that sex belongs to our lower nature seem thoroughly gone. Sex is wholly good if done in intimacy, and mostly harmless in other contexts. One-night stands still happen, and they are pardoned as excusable, almost inevitable. However, one-night stands are far from the ideal. A person searches for that fragile state of intimacy wherein sexual intercourse is an expression of caring. There and then, sex is a gift from heaven.

2. *The independent individual.* Always, even within intimate relationships, two watchful individuals retain their independence. They consider their own needs paramount. Picking at random a copy of *Glamour*, I find Bette-Jane Raphael writing, "I believe that we all have the right to decide what to disclose to our partners. Some relationships are more open than others, but that doesn't necessarily affect how they finally fare.

"No one, not even my partner, is entitled to know everything about me. Why should he know that I once stole crayons from Woolworth's when I was a little girl?"

In the same issue, in a monthly column entitled "Sexual Ethics," Priscilla Grant writes, "True lovers give each other permission to retreat; no lengthy explanations or excuses are necessary."

Intimacy, by the new ethic, never controls the individual; the individual always remains free. No covenant binds one person to another through absolute obligations. An individual's primary covenant is always to him- or herself.

3. *Compatibility.* If you ask what creates intimacy, the answer, in a word, is "compatibility." This does not particularly mean sexual compatibility. Time was when the rationale for couples sleeping together before marriage was "How else will they know whether they are sexually compatible?" By now, though, nearly everyone knows that couples are not sexually incompatible as a Ford transmission is incompatible with a Honda drive train. They are compatible or incompatible in personality and values.

Nonetheless, this is usually seen as compatibility that just happens—you "click." Of course, people do change over time, so couples who are compatible today may not click tomorrow. That is why you cannot be rigidly opposed to divorce or adultery. Few favor divorce or adultery, but against incompatibility, who can stand? Happy, lifelong monogamy is less a triumph of the will than a miracle of compatibility. You hope that you and your lover can stay balanced on the bubble indefinitely. But you admit that the forces of fate may ruin your plans.

4. *Sex is a private matter.* Sex under the Ethic of Intimacy society, then, has nothing to do with it. What you do and whom you do it with is a matter for you to settle for yourself. The Moral Majority can live how they please, but they have no right to tell others how to behave. A person's sexual behavior is his or her own business—unless that person happens to be running for President. Thus, a church that expels a member for sexual misconduct can be sued, and many people believe it should be, for they see sexual conduct as none of the church's business.

The privatization of sex received a huge boost when penicillin and the Pill came out of the laboratories. Both fostered what can now clearly be labeled an illusion: that sex, thanks to medical breakthroughs, has no impact on society. In an era of millions of abortions, of multiple generations of unwed mothers on public support, of epidemic sexually transmitted diseases, the idea that sex is a strictly private matter is incredible. Yet it continues to exert a powerful force.

5. *Sex has no necessary personal consequences.* The Old Consensus treated the move from virginity to sexual experience as a change in a person's very being. Today people think the impact of sex is almost

infinitely variable. Intercourse is thought to mean different things to different people at different times. Whether a person is a virgin or not, whether he or she has had one partner or dozens, tells you very little about that individual.

According to the Ethic of Intimacy, virginity is a meaningless mystification used to keep "good girls" good. Some people have bad sexual experiences, but with counseling they should be able to get over these. Guilt feelings are not necessary. The broad assumption is: Most people will have sex with numbers of people while trying to "click." Even when the relationship is a failure, at least they are learning about life. They are getting to know their own sexual responses. Some experiences will be good and others not-so-good. But every time, with every new partner, you have a chance to start afresh. The past is merely prologue, not predictor.

6. *No double standard.* Today women are treated exactly the same as men, sexually. If sexual feelings are right for one, they are right for the other. If you wink at one's roving, you should wink at the other's.

7. *Sex requires maturity.* The Ethic of Intimacy is situational; each person must consider a number of variables in knowing what to do; and what is right for one person in a particular situation might not be right for another.

But applying situation ethics requires maturity and wisdom, especially when sex and its emotions are involved. Many people doubt whether kids are capable of it. They feel uneasy about this doubt because of point 4: *Sex is a private matter.* What right do they have to impose their opinions on anybody, even children? Ellen Goodman, writing in *Ms.* magazine about the ambivalence of parents trying to convey a new morality to their kids, quoted a woman with a 13-year-old daughter as saying, "We're trying to communicate a situational norm, like, it's okay under certain circumstances. If you both honest-to-God want to. If you think you'll be in each other's lives for a while. If you are responsible. If you use birth control, if you are old enough, if you won't get hurt, if you have a wholesome sexual experience." Commented Goodman, "Her list of 'ifs' extends into the air."

Despite this uncertainty, an uneasy consensus has emerged that kids 16 and under are too young for sex, and should be told so. (This consensus, however, is consistently undermined by the contention championed by Planned Parenthood—that widespread sexual activity is inevitable among teenagers, and that however much adults might like teenagers under 17 to stop engaging in sex, they will continue. Therefore, the only sensible course of action is to dispense contraceptives and abortions freely.)

Susan works as a paralegal assistant in a suburban law firm. Divorced for three years, she has two children in elementary school. This week they are with their father, and it is sheer relief. Raising kids alone is no picnic.

The law firm has provided Susan's only stability through dizzying changes. When her marriage broke up, the firm's partners, Randy and Dave, offered to take her on full-time at a good salary. They are flexible about her hours, too.

Besides their economic consideration, both partners have become friends. A lot of good-natured kidding and flirting goes on at the office, and it helps Susan relax. She feels needed and appreciated there, which she just about never feels when she is at home.

Today, when Randy is leaving for a lunch appointment, he pops his head in her door. "Hey, I was thinking," he says. "Your kids are gone for the week, right? Why don't we go out to dinner tonight and have some fun?" Her surprise must show. "Don't look so shocked," he says. "I'll check with you when I come back, right?"

A lot of their office kidding centers around Randy's love life. He is not particularly handsome, but with his easy charm he never lacks for companionship. He is unmarried. Susan has liked him for a long time.

She is not a prude. She thinks of herself as somewhat typical of women her age. Starting when she was a junior in high school, she always slept with her boyfriends. Not that there were so many of them. One in high school; they split when he joined the navy. Three in college. She was in love with each one of them; only once, on a weekend ski trip, did she have a fling with a stranger, and she vowed not to repeat the experience. Her senior year she met Pete, and the day before graduation he asked her to marry him. They lasted six years, and she was faithful to him throughout.

Since the divorce she has been out a few times, but generally she is too tired to meet men. Those she's met haven't been very appealing, either. But Randy? It doesn't take long for her imagination to go to work. She could use some romance in her life, she tells herself. It has been a long time.

Then, like the shadow of a bird, the thought of AIDS passes through her mind. It disturbs her, and she tries to put it away. She will have to get some condoms, she supposes, and she wonders whether Randy will like that. Her husband hated them. But knowing Randy's lifestyle there is no question but that "safe sex" is indicated.

A few months ago a man with AIDS came into their office to do a will. He was paper thin. The office became quieter than a library. They say the incubation period for the virus might be ten years, or more. How many women (And men? She doesn't think so.) has Randy been with in the last ten years? Thirty? At least that many, she thinks. Susan's imagination traces the path backward to all those partners, and all their partners, and all their partners, back and back and back for ten years. Her small office becomes quite crowded with these shadowy presences until, in annoyance, she shoos them away and goes back to her paperwork. It is an extremely unpleasant way to think.

AIDS has brought a slight hesitation to America's headlong pursuit of sexual happiness, like a shudder barely felt from below when two straining tectonic plates slip. Some people feel nothing; others lift their heads with a quizzical expression, as though to say, "Did I imagine that?"

AIDS has done what ten thousand urgent moralists (myself included) have failed to do: make secular society wonder, "Do we really know what we are doing?" America's sexual revolution had been a children's crusade, full of good feeling and hope that once the wicked witch of sexual repression was dead, all would be well. The optimism is still plentiful, but there is just enough of a hesitation right now that another point of view may possibly be heard.

Yet it is only a hesitation. Psychologist Kaye Cook reports that she reads much more about committed relationships, but sees no dramatic change in behavior. Rather, people continue to sleep with a variety of partners and to hope that commitment will somehow evolve. A recent *Cosmopolitan* magazine poll found women saying that in the era of AIDS, they had changed their lifestyle. Only 1 percent would now go to bed with a man on the first date (25 percent had in the past). However, 71 percent would go to bed on the third or fourth date. Some change!

Susan fears AIDS. Her life has been lightly touched by its influence. But what will she do with Randy? She will almost certainly go to bed with him. AIDS she can still shoo away. Her loneliness, her sexual desire, are much more real.

Even in the gay community, where life and death are clearly at stake, the levels of sexual promiscuity, while diminished, continue to be astonishing. Sex is a powerful impulse, and is rarely stopped by mere terror. Hundreds of years of syphilis did not put prostitutes out of business, either. You can grow used to terror, as residents of Beirut know.

Moreover, the fundamental context for sexuality has not changed. The latest crop of pop sex experts speak less of the joy of 56 sexual positions, and more of the makings (and breakings) of a relationship. However, they continue to write as pragmatists dedicated to the autonomous individual searching for a way that "works for him." Morality, sacrifice, sin and guilt, if they are mentioned at all, are personal prejudices that no one (least of all a psychologist) would impose on another. The Ethic of Intimacy is still going strong in the era of AIDS.

The victims
What can we say about the Ethic of Intimacy? Should we shout frantic warnings about the dangers of AIDS? That seems unlikely to work—and likely to backfire, if a cure is found.

Then what can we say? Christians can hardly be against intimacy. We value it too. What we must say, I think, is that the Ethic of Intimacy is too weak—too weak to deal with the powerful human urges, often destructive, always potential, that make up our sexuality. It is like walking a lion on a leash. Sometimes he goes where you want him to. Sometimes he will not. Sometimes he turns around and devours you.

The Ethic of Intimacy is inherently vague; under the sway of emotions you can convince yourself anything is intimate. And there is a strange current of passivity and fatalism in it—a surrendering of self to the gods of eros—which undermines human dignity. For if compatibility is the key to intimacy, we are at the mercy of circumstance. Either we are with the right one—or we have missed and must start over.

It is a strange paradox that modern people, who insist on their sexual freedom, can think of no way to use their freedom other than changing partners. The Christian ideal places a person's will at the center: Love is work to be done, and intimacy is to be created through persistent self-sacrifice. The Ethic of Intimacy puts our efforts in a much-less-important place.

Because of these weaknesses, the Ethic of Intimacy does not live up to its own standards. It does not create or enhance intimacy. It merely glorifies it.

Christians have, as well, a religious concern about the Ethic of Intimacy. A pure and loving monogamy reflects a pure love of God. As the Book of Ephesians tells us, husband and wife are like Christ and his church. We must train ourselves to have what Letha Scanzoni calls "the single eye," both toward our spouse and toward our Lord. If we lose this singularity in marriage, we will at the least lose a way of understanding our relationship with God.

But modern people are not much interested in knowing how their sexuality influences their relationship to God. If someone asks what is wrong with the Ethic of Intimacy in secular terms, I would say simply, "There are too many victims." I would say, "Six hundred thousand babies born each year to teenagers, many of whom will spend their lives in poverty. One-and-a-half million abortions. Twelve million cases of sexually transmitted diseases (many incurable, some deadly). Millions upon millions of divorces; millions upon millions of children growing up with one parent. About three times as many divorced women now as in the seventies. (Divorced men remarry women on the average ten years younger than the wives they divorced. The older women have a much smaller chance to remarry.) And on the whole, there is less intimacy and more loneliness than ever before."

All these statistics are regularly in the newspapers. Societally we are reeling: burdened with an underclass of ruined families, staggered by millions of abortions, and terrified by sexual epidemics. The wide-eyed promises of the sexual revolution, that all would be well once Victorianism was uprooted, can hardly be made with a straight face any more. Yet nobody (except shouting, perspiring fundamentalist evangelists on TV) seems to put cause and effect together.

We manage to shrug off the victims because they are mostly people who "don't matter"—the poor, the young, the uneducated, the slightly-too-old women. And the damage is diffuse. Not everybody suffers. Plenty of people sleep together before marriage, even live together before marriage, and yet form strong, durable relationships. Homosexuals make outstanding, sober-minded citizens. Men and women leave their families to form new marriages, and seem to gain peace of mind.

Some do, that is. Many don't. Only an extraordinary, willed amnesia enables us to forget millions of victims.

Our society regards them as unavoidable. Experts stress the medical cures, the legal and economic reforms that minimize the pain. Certainly minimizing pain is right. But the huge number of casualties is not inevitable. There have been few times in all history, in fact, when so many sexual casualties have been present in any society.

How the Ethic of Intimacy affects teenagers

A critical test of any ethical system, particularly regarding sexuality, is how it affects the young. They are highly vulnerable, for with them nothing is settled. And they are our future. How does the Ethic of Intimacy filter down to them?

Personally, I have found much of the pathos of our situation in the thousands of letters from kids I read. I have also kept up on sociological statistics about teenage sexuality. In this chapter I rely primarily on statistics found in the recent study *Sex and the American Teenager*, by Robert Coles and Geoffrey Stokes. Other studies show similar results. The Ethic of Intimacy does percolate down to teenagers, and it leads to experiences I think are very unlikely to foster lifelong intimacy.

1. *An invariably positive view of sex* reinforces what needs no encouragement—kids' interest in sex. Kids get the message that sex is wonderful and right whenever two people are intimate. They assume this includes them, since at age 13 more than half say they have been in love, and by age 17 or 18 over 80 percent believe they have already experienced love.

Few teenagers are truly promiscuous, sleeping with just anyone. Two-thirds experience sex for the first time with their boyfriend or girlfriend. Once they begin they nearly always continue. Only 6 percent of the nonvirgins surveyed had gone for more than a year since last having intercourse. This means very few have only one or two experiences of sexual intercourse and then quit.

Why do they continue? Because they like it. Many of the girls experience disappointment or pain initially, but ultimately, about two-thirds of both boys and girls who have had sex report enjoying intercourse either "a great deal" or "a large amount." Thus the Ethic of Intimacy is experienced: Intimate sex is good—at least it feels good, and it certainly feels intimate. This is so regardless of their moral or religious viewpoints. Consider this letter I recently received:

I am 22 years old, and until a month ago I was a virgin. I admit my virginity was a frail one, one in flesh only because I'd thought about making love so much.

What bothers me is that my heart is so apathetic. I love my Lord and have witnessed his work. I know he is alive and in my heart, and I believe his word, but when it comes time to go see my present boyfriend, I feel nothing holds me back. I enjoy making love to him very much.

When I come home at 2:00 A.M. from his apartment, I begin to feel remorse and know I am hurting my God. But the next day it's gone.

Such liaisons are not loveless. About half the 15-year-old girls expect to marry their most recent sexual partners. (Boys seem more realistic: 82 percent said they did *not* plan to marry their partners. Evidently their sense of intimacy did not necessarily include telling their partners this fact.) Unfortunately, almost none of them will.

2. *The independent individual* means that these kids experience a series of short relationships. Indeed, independent individuals of all ages are less likely to stick together, since they have no overarching loyalty to hold them together. This tendency, however, is far more pronounced in teenagers, because they are rapidly changing, because they move when their parents do, and because many eventually go away to college. Only 14 percent of teenagers' sexual relationships last more than a year—about as many as last a week. Since half the sexually active teenagers start sexual relationships in their early teens, they run up quite a string of sexual partners. One need not conclude that these relationships are unimportant, or the breakups relatively painless. One staple letter I receive is from the teenager trying to get over a relationship, agonizing about it and fantasizing over it as many as two or three years later. We have no instruments to measure pain, but my impression is that these kids feel as devastated as do adults in divorce court.

3. *Compatibility* brings an almost frantic concern with finding "the right one." Letter after letter comes to me asking for formulas: How do I find the right one? How do I know if I have found him? How can I tell if this is true love or merely infatuation? Kids have long had fantasies about meeting "Mr. Right," but they daydreamed at a relatively harmless level. Today they go to bed together. They lack a future orientation, toward which they dream and pine and mentally prepare. They think, like their parents, more existentially. If you happen upon the right person, you can be intimate. It is more a matter of being at the right place at the right time than a matter of choosing one sterling person to love for life. Commitment and character decrease in importance if compatibility is crucial.

4. *Sex is a private matter* means that kids have a tremendous amount of respect for others' decisions. Take this letter:

A friend recently confided in me that her boyfriend and she have been sexually active for almost a year. Because we are close friends, I want to be supportive of her, but I'm not sure how right it is for me not to discourage her from making love with someone whom she says she loves. I know I have no right to control her morals. It was hard to answer when she asked me whether or not I thought it was "wrong"— because what I may consider wrong for myself may not apply to her.

A sizable minority of kids hope to stay virgins until they marry, but they usually consider this a purely idiosyncratic decision. On one hand, these kids benefit from sexual privacy: Their peers might razz them a little, but usually not much. (Here I am talking about public pressures. Between a boy and a girl alone, a good deal of pressure can be applied.) On the other hand, privacy means that kids feel very strongly that sex is *their* decision, and none of their parents' or their teachers' or their pastors' or even their friends' business. Society's collective caution disappears. Sexual and romantic urges gain in significance.

5. *Sex has no necessary consequences* means that kids are often confounded by their own experiences when they find consequences, emotional or physical, staring at them.

Many do experience physical consequences—pregnancy or disease. But not many 16-year-olds have thought beforehand about what it would be like to have herpes for life. A tone of astonishment and shame pervades their letters when they write to me after discovering that they have an incurable disease. Their own physical suffering is only one part of their regret. They cannot imagine how they will someday tell a person they want to marry.

Even more common are psychological consequences, among which is the fact that once they have begun participating in sex, many find they cannot stop.

I have a big problem. About four years ago I met a really nice guy who had just moved to my neighborhood. He was the first guy I really loved, and the first guy who really loved me back. We started going together about six months after he moved here. We had a very serious relationship—we were sexually active.

We broke up one year ago, and we're still sexually active. We still care about each other a lot, but not enough to be doing this. Besides, it's wrong.

He goes away to college this fall. I don't know if that's good or bad, because I couldn't imagine never seeing him again. I still care about him a lot. He's my best friend. I'm very jealous of him and other girls he sees or dates. I feel I have a right to be.

I want to be happy, but it's been so long since I have been! We've tried to stop having sex, but so far it hasn't worked. I've prayed, but nothing seems to help. I don't have anyone to talk to. I have learned a lesson, though: sex can be a very bad habit, if you start when you aren't with the person you will be spending the rest of your life with.

When teenagers surrender their virginity, their lives are changed. If they once imagined themselves sleeping only with the love of their life, they now usually must adjust to the reality that they will have a number of sexual partners. By the time they get married, they will have a sexual history to tell. Poignantly, 15 percent of the girls who have begun having intercourse say they had wanted to be virgins when they married.

6. *The end of the double standard.* Teenagers today make no distinction between the morality of girls and boys—even though their parents often still do. No doubt this is a good development. Nonetheless, those who become sexually active still encounter the double standard of biology. Only about half the sexually active teenagers use birth control, which means that somewhere between

10 percent to 40 percent of all American girls get pregnant while they are teenagers. Many of them have abortions, and the experience is often traumatic. Those who keep their babies usually drop out of school and often end up dependent on welfare or their parents or both. Though the boy often sticks with the girl through the immediate trauma, teenage relationships almost never endure beyond the crisis. Girls continue to be victims, with or without the double standard.

7. *Sex requires maturity* suggests that kids are not ready to experience sex—at least in their early teens. But the weakness of a situation ethic shows up: Those least capable of mastering a situation ethic are often most likely to believe themselves capable. Nobody yet has managed to convince a majority of teenagers that an experience that is right for 25-year-olds is wrong for 15-year-olds. That sounds too arbitrary. Besides, it is probably in the nature of teenagerdom to believe yourself fully grown up.

Consequently, the adult consensus of 16 or younger being too young for sex has made no observable impact. At 15, a quarter of the teenage population, both boys and girls, have already had intercourse.

The new double standard
Any ethical framework must be judged, not by how it works with the strongest members of society, but by how it works with the most vulnerable. Those supporting the Ethic of Intimacy would like to have a double standard: one for teenagers, another for adults. This does not work.

Not everyone sees the situation among adolescents so balefully. Kathryn Burkhart, in *Growing into Love: Teenagers Talk Candidly About Sex in the 1980s*, states the optimistic case. "Making explorations into their sexual feelings and into sexual interactions with another person at the age of 16 or 18 does not mean that today's teenagers will be any better or worse off than we were when we did the same things at the ages of 20 or 25. Some of them will make right choices for themselves, and some will make wrong choices. They will have relationships that affect them in a variety of ways. But when they behave sexually, when they respond to another person, they are doing something that human beings have done for as far back as the history of humans extends itself. Even though each sexual experience is individual and intimate and unique, in it, we become part of the human race, linked to humankind, past and future, regardless of what language we speak, what customs, beliefs, cultures, attitudes, or perspectives we bring to the experience.

"Today's teenagers may be aware earlier, they may be exposed to more, they may make decisions sooner than they would otherwise, but they'll most likely find their way through the hazards and the squalls and the ways of the world as well as we did. And in their own way."

Burkhart also gives her prescription for teenage ethics: "It seems to me that adolescents of all ages should be encouraged to have foreplay and to defer intercourse until they are extremely comfortable in their own bodies and very much at ease about themselves and their sexual partners. Teenagers should think about their own requirements for sexual intimacy and have great respect for their own feelings and values."

Her words are an excellent reflection of the vagueness of the Ethic of Intimacy. The great reassurance, phrased in the rosy glow of organic unity, is that people have been having sex for a long time, and that these kids are doing it, too. The values kids should follow are that they are to be "extremely comfortable in their own bodies," "at ease about themselves," "aware of their own requirements," and to "respect their own feelings and values." In two words: "Be careful." I leave you to guess what this will tell a kid after a half-hour in the back bedroom.

This is no proof that we are seeing the first sign of the decline and fall of the West. Teenagers still believe in marriage; a lot of them (perhaps half the girls) hope to be virgins at the wedding. The family is a durable institution, and history indicates it has survived worse enemies than vague ethical standards.

But no one can doubt that there will be many more casualties, particularly among the most vulnerable members of society. Already it is clear that kids from divorced families are almost twice as likely to engage in sex as teenagers whose parents have remained together. It is not difficult to imagine that these same kids will form weak marriages and that, in turn, their kids will have a long series of sexual partners culminating in more weak marriages. I am not suggesting that people who engage in premarital sex are necessarily any worse morally than their peers who do not. I am asserting that those who build their sexual lives around the vagueness of intimacy will be less likely to build strong marriages. To build strong marriages—a difficult thing under the best of circumstances—you must put marriage at the top of your sexual values. I would also assert that strong marriages offer the greatest possibilities for true and lasting intimacy.

For lack of a counterculture

The strongest predictor of whether teenagers will have sexual intercourse is whether they are influenced either "a large amount" or "a great deal" by religion. About 18 percent of kids say they are, and only 10 percent of them have had intercourse. This is not, as noted above, a matter of nominal religion. It is a question of how they themselves have responded to God. In this committed minority we find, perhaps, the beginnings of a counterculture.

Few kids will buck the Ethic of Intimacy with no belief system to substitute for it. A child from a family that can articulate, in word and deed, a pure, loving monogamy will have a strong reason to want to center his or her sexual hopes on marriage. A teenager who becomes, by personal choice, a member of a Christian community that articulates the same thing will have equally strong reasons.

I fear, though, that many Christians have almost fallen for the Ethic of Intimacy. In responding to the Playboy experiment, we have put great emphasis on the joys of love, and we have unconsciously downplayed the institution of marriage. We have become sympathetic to divorce—not merely compassionate toward those who divorce, but sympathetic to the reasons why they do it. We have acknowledged that marriage can be very difficult, but we have not said much about what benefit justifies this difficulty. We have collaborated with the emphasis on compatibility by building a theology of "the right one," whom we say God will reveal through a sense of inner peace. We have communicated to our children our fear of premarital sex (though we still, strangely, sprawl in front of the TV, where by one count, six extramarital sex encounters are portrayed for every one of sex between spouses). But we have not communicated, I think, the great value of marriage, an institution that demands so much of us in such clear, hard lines.

The Ethic of Intimacy is destructive for adults as well as teenagers, and in the same ways. It simply is not strong enough to train our wild, contradictory, variable sexual and romantic impulses; it works, rather, to help us justify doing what we wish. For some—particularly the attractive, the well-off, and those in their twenties and thirties—this freedom will be pleasant. But for society as a whole, and particularly among the less attractive, the poor, the very young, or the too old, the Ethic of Intimacy creates too many victims. And even those who seem to thrive do less well than they ought: They should be learning how to deepen love in the face of difficulties, rather than merely enjoying the freedom to "click."

The appeal of marriage lies in its toughness, in its rigorous, invariable demand that each individual choose one person, and one only, to marry, and in its demand that each one sacrifice to create within that marriage a garden of intimacy. Make no mistake: A pure, loving monogamy forces us to do things we would rather not. Its sternness may never be a fountain of popular songs. But we need its strength and clarity to drive the powerful force of our sexuality toward lasting intimacy.

It has never been easy to communicate or maintain a belief that demands such commitment. The challenge posed for us by the Ethic of Intimacy, I believe, is not only to preach to teenagers against premarital sex, but to preach to people of all ages the immense value of a pure and loving monogamy, and to live it so well as to make it attractive.

Chapter 2

SEXUAL SALVATION IN MODERN AMERICA

*T*he drums exploded and the songs of the singers rose to heaven as two priests from the interior of the temple led forth a priestess clothed in white. It was the moment that Urbaal had been awaiting—for this was the slave girl, tall and most radiantly beautiful. Standing at the edge of the temple steps, she kept her hands folded and her eyes downcast while the priest signaled for the music to cease, whereupon priestly hands began taking away her garments, one by one, allowing them to fall like petals until she stood naked for the approval of the town.

She was an exquisite human being, a perfection of the goddess Astarte, for no man could look at her provocative form without seeing in her the sublime representation of fertility. She was a girl whose purpose was to be loved, to be taken away and made fertile so that she could reproduce her grandeur and bless the earth. Urbaal stared with unbelieving eyes as the naked girl submitted herself to the crowd's inspection. . . .

"She is Libamah," the priest in charge announced, "servant of Astarte, and soon in the month of harvest she will go to the man who *has this year produced the best, whether it be barley or olives or cattle or any growth of the soil."*

"Let it be me," Urbaal whispered hoarsely. Clenching his fists, he prayed to all his [gods]. "Let it be me. . . ."

The priest raised his arms in blessing over the naked girl, then lowered them slowly to indicate that singing was wanted, and the musicians began a hushed chant to which the tall girl started quietly to dance. Keeping her head lowered, she moved her arms and knees in seductive rhythms, increasing the tempo of her movements as the drums grew more prominent. Soon her feet were apart, and she was gyrating in taunting patterns until the men of the audience were biting their lips in hunger. . . .

"In the month of harvest," the priest shouted to the crowd, "she will belong to one of you." Quickly his assistants covered her tall form with the discarded clothes, and whisked her from sight. The crowd groaned, even the women, for they had hoped to see a more complete ceremony; but the steps were not empty for long: four well-known priestesses were led forth—many men had known these four—and they too were stripped naked, revealing far less inviting bodies than Libamah's, but symbols of fertility nevertheless. With no delay the priests nominated four towns-men to join the priestesses, and the citizens—lucky or unlucky as the case might be—left their wives and leaped up the steps. Each grabbed for the woman designated for him, leading her to the chambers set aside for this periodic rite.

"Through them life will be born again!" the chorus chanted. . . .
—James A. Michener, *The Source*

The first chapter looked at the sexual revolution from a pragmatic point of view. How does it affect ordinary lives? Does it live up to its promises? James Michener's portrayal of ancient fertility religion reminds us that sex has always raised deeper issues than mere practicality. Sex is tied to the human search for meaning and transcendence. On that basis, as well as for a pragmatic reason, the sexual revolution must be evaluated.

The Pill and penicillin triggered the sexual revolution, but in and of themselves they do not explain it. After all, the Pill and penicillin are available worldwide, but not all societies have followed our lead toward sexual liberalism. China and Iran, for instance, have become far stricter. Technological advances made the sexual revolution feasible, but some deeper impulse had to drive it.

The Pill and penicillin did not develop in a vacuum, as though an Einstein musing in his laboratory suddenly conceived them out of nothing. They were developed through years of cooperative effort at great expense because of deeply felt societal desires. Penicillin could only be discovered and developed by a society deeply committed to curing disease—that is, to controlling certain effects of nature. The Pill could only be developed by a society fascinated by sexuality as a subject for medical investigation—and thus committed to controlling sexuality (as a part of nature). Our society, more than any before, is committed to a relentless scientific probing of nature, not simply in order to understand nature, but in order to control and transform it.

This holds true in genetics (we cannot be content to understand our genetic makeup, we must master gene splicing) and atomic physics (not merely the understanding of the universe, but nuclear power and bombs), and no less does it hold true of sexuality. Masters and Johnson not only studied the functioning of the clitoris, they pioneered "sex therapy." Medical doctors, however, had been involved in trying to fix sex before. It is no accident that medical doctors far more than priests and pastors led hysterical Victorian attempts to stop masturbation, and they are equally at the forefront of twentieth-century attempts to use masturbation as a tool to help people have a better sex life. The two attempts mirror each other. Both combine intensely serious "scientific" study of sexuality, and the determined attempt to control and use it. Whether abhorring or cultivating masturbation, study and control are used to make life wonderful.

The sexual revolution represents a revolution in confidence. The Pill and penicillin gave confidence that we could master disease and reproduction. Freud, or pop-Freud, gave confidence that we could control sexual guilt. A surge of post–World War II egalitarianism gave confidence that men and women need not be limited by their gender. Suddenly, humankind seemed really able to choose without limit: to do whatever it wanted with whomever it wanted, without having to fit into a rigid framework instituted by nature or God. Oh yes, God. It was necessary to have confidence about him, too: either that he had evolved into a benign, smiling dignitary, or that he had ceased to exist altogether.

Why this new thing?

The theme of autonomous mastery ("You will be like God") is not a new one, of course. Since Adam and Eve, human beings have been experimenting with ways to make God superfluous. Nonetheless, the sexual revolution is something new under the sun. Historians and anthropologists increasingly recognize its uniqueness. Princeton historian Lawrence Stone writes, "Before now, sexual libertinism has been confined to narrow elite circles, often around a court. Its dissemination among a population at large, as has occurred in the last 20 years, is a phenomenon unique in the history of developed societies."

Historians do not use the word *unique* lightly. Some undeveloped societies—notably in Polynesia—apparently institutionalized promiscuous premarital sex, it is true. (Margaret Mead eulogized this in her famous, flawed book on Samoa—a classic example of social science producing what society wants to hear.) But this happened only among some undeveloped, tribal societies. A consistent mark of developed societies is that they value premarital virginity and strongly protect the bond of marriage. Our society, alone in history, is attempting to change this.

Why this new thing? Some claim that our uniqueness comes because we are the first generation to have effective birth control. Before, extramarital sex meant children born out of marriage; now, sex is freed from that constraint. "After centuries of guilt and repression, the bait of sexual pleasure has at long last been separated from the hook of reproduction. We finally have acquired sexual freedom," claims Irene Kassorla in *Nice Girls Do*. But it is increasingly obvious that the Pill has not eliminated the "hook" of unwanted pregnancies; there are now more unwanted children (as well as abortions) than ever in our history. Nor, when you think about it, is it apparent why pregnancy has to contend against sexual fulfillment. Not all societies have thought of pregnancy and sexual pleasure as implacable rivals. Some might say that the possibility of children is one of the chief pleasures of sex.

There is another common explanation for the new approach of our age: It is really not new at all, but merely the return to a normal way of thinking about sex. According to this hypothesis, what was "new" was the vicious censorship and moral hysteria of earlier times. Victorian prudishness, it is commonly said, brought massive repression, and our twentieth-century sexual revolution is merely a counterreaction against it.

This hypothesis, however, does not match the historical evidence. The French historian Michel Foucault, in his multivolume history of sexuality, makes a convincing case that Victorian sexual moralizing and our twentieth-century sexual revolution are only different facets of a consistent, growing attention to sex (or, more exactly, to talking and confessing about sex) that began more than two centuries ago. We have not, Foucault claims, returned to a pre-Victorian approach to sex; we have carried on the Victorian obsession with sex, only in a different way.

Historian Peter Gardella makes a further point about the nineteenth-century American doctors and religious figures who pronounced on sexuality, stigmatizing masturbation and suggesting that, ideally, married couples should have intercourse once a year. These men and women are usually presented as moss-grown conservatives. In fact, Gardella says, they were from the most liberal, optimistic strand of society. They expected medicine (which included programs of sexual control and diet) would do through a scientific health program what the church in centuries of preaching had been unable to do: make people good. Essentially, their intentions were not very different from those of modern-day sex experts; only their technique was different. A vast, deep cultural movement has long been under way: a movement to study, understand, and control our sexuality in order to save ourselves.

Sex transcending nature
People sometimes describe the sexual revolution as an attempt to get back to "natural" sex. But even a casual glance at the current literature of sexuality will show that it is at certain points extremely opposed to anything natural. For instance, if you listen to Dr. Ruth, you will hear her obsessively ask her callers whether or not they use birth control. She writes, "I would like this country to put its resources toward finding a perfect contraceptive. . . . Good contraception is important for the peace of mind people need in order to abandon themselves into the never-never land of sexual excitement and pleasure and ecstasy without having to worry that somebody may get pregnant. It is foolish to allow the danger of an unwanted pregnancy to enter into the lovemaking experience. . . ."

Many experts in sexuality would agree with Dr. Ruth. Fear of unwanted pregnancy clearly can interfere with the pleasures of recreational sex. But even more clearly, we are not then talking about "natural" sex. Pregnancy goes naturally with sex, if anything does. The sexual revolution is not a revolution against an unnatural view of sex; it is a revolution in favor of a studied, calculatedly unnatural sexuality. The need for endless volumes on technique, for unnumbered clinics run by scientific "sex therapists," for monthly educational articles in *Reader's Digest*, to say nothing of our fascination with movie images of beautiful individuals pretending to have intercourse—all this makes very obvious that our age is not at all interested in letting sex take its blessedly natural course, but in stimulating it, studying it, teaching it, therapizing it, and controlling it until it meets some ideal. It is no longer credible to claim that we are temporarily concerned with overturning the rigid proscriptions of Victorianism, and that once we have purged ourselves of moralistic poison, our fascination with sex will decline to some healthy, normal level. Year after year the concern, the anxiety, the fascination with sex grow.

Foucault writes that we have come "to direct the question of what we are, to sex." Gardella puts it more broadly (and perhaps more as an American): "Our sexual ethic has a religious quality that it could only have inherited from the Christian zeal to overcome sin and to experience salvation. As Tom Wolfe observed, Americans seek in orgasm 'a spark of the Divine.' "

Why the sexual revolution? Perhaps, as Christian belief has faded, another faith has been needed to take its place. Science and the social sciences have served in this quest for meaning, but they have not provided the fundamental direction. They have taken their cues, as good servants of society, from a fundamental shift of view. Western society, which once viewed sex as a source of danger, at its best confined to marriage and used for the production of children, now views sex as a source of limitless pleasure and personal discovery, at its best freed from the inhibiting possibility of children or any other social consideration. If in the past sex was unrealistically viewed as demonic, it is now viewed as messianic. We study sex as a savior: It will tell us our true nature and save us from meaninglessness.

Sex and religion
Sex as savior has an astonishing quality to it. C. S. Lewis caught it

when he wrote, "You can get a large audience together for a strip-tease act—that is, to watch a girl undress on a stage. Now suppose you came to a country where you could fill a theatre by simply bringing a covered plate on to the stage and then slowly lifting the cover so as to let every one see, just before the lights went out, that it contained a mutton chop or a piece of bacon. . . ."

Such behavior would show, Lewis said, that something had gone wrong with people's appetite for food. But there is a subtler implication. It would be strange for people to crowd into a room to see a piece of bacon uncovered, but perhaps no stranger than what one sees in any Christian church when people take Communion, lovingly holding and distributing tiny bits of bread and drops of wine. In religion, simple things become infused with a greater meaning. They gain a fascination and an emotional importance far beyond their practical function. So it is with sex in our time: It has become a sacrament.

If it seems strange to speak of sex in such language, that is a heritage of Western society. Much more common has been a close link between religion and sexuality. Andrew Greeley writes, "The most fundamental insight that primitive man had about sexuality is one that we frequently overlook or forget: that it is a raw, primal, basic power over which we have only very limited control. Primitive man invariably viewed sexuality as sacred, because for him the 'sacred' was the 'powerful,' and sexuality was one of the fundamental forces that kept the universe going."

From this to the fertility cult, which Michener portrayed so graphically in *The Source,* is only a short step. The fertility cults were apparently born in Mesopotamia, and for centuries operated alongside the religion of the Old Testament. (The prophets denounced their people's "prostitution," literal and figurative, when Israelites accepted fertility religion as a complement to their own faith.) Fertility cults were also an active influence in Greek culture during the New Testament era, particularly in Corinth.

Because our Christian heritage condemned such sex religions, we have been shielded from their influence. Westerners may think that sex religions are a strange variation on "normal" religion. The truth is more the opposite. Most of the world's great religions placed sex—often extramarital sex—in a central, sacramental position. How did they manage this while still emphasizing premarital virginity and decrying adultery? Often they did it through a well-organized system of concubines and temple prostitutes, which operated on a parallel, noncompeting basis with marriage. Concubines and prostitutes were not necessarily despised women with no other options in life. On the contrary, they were often respected, educated, honored women. When British missionaries to India first started schools for young women, many Indians assumed that they must be training prostitutes for Christian worship since prostitutes were the only Indian women to receive an education.

Hinduism, of all the great living religions, is most directly a descendant of the fertility worship Michener dramatized. Until this century, temple prostitution was an active, respected aspect of worship in India. Hindu temples are often decorated with sculptures depicting copulation; religious parades carry large phalluses. There is nothing dirty about sex in Hinduism; instead, there is something sacred and powerful, something that brings you into contact with the gods.

The oldest forms of Buddhism, by contrast, have a strongly ascetic cast; monks are celibate. But over centuries, Buddhism came to take different forms, and Tantric Buddhism made even more of sex than Hinduism did. Group orgies were a form of union with the gods.

Taoism and Confucianism, more philosophic than theistic, viewed the male-female balance—yin-yang—as fundamental, and thus the proper sexual relations as religiously crucial. A man observed a very careful sexual regimen with his wives and concubines, being careful to absorb as much yin (female) essence as possible while conserving his own yang (male) essence. The result of this quasi-scientific sexual regimen was supposed to be perfect harmony.

In all these, and in other less-known religions, it was very natural for people to think of sexual energy as related to a divine, life-giving energy.

Sex religion in the twentieth century

Are these religions different from the religion of sex in the twentieth century? Obviously they are, in many different ways. The sexual revolution is explicitly secular, and many of its experts would be scandalized to think of themselves as promoting a religious view. But one does not need much imagination to see that the sexual revolution attempts to recast reality so that sexual experiences can give meaning to ordinary life. That sort of enterprise is just what religion is about.

Historical theologian William Stafford writes, "Hugh Hefner's career is a graphic example of how far this creation of reality may need to go. Inventing a 'philosophy' to rearrange his own values and relationships was straightforward enough. Then came the magazine, the houses, the clubs, as a sort of monastic order for 'free sex,' where an entire culture of voyeurism and sexual play could flourish, where other perspectives could not interrupt the constant stimulation. The order was quite evangelistic; few Americans' values are now unmarked by the Playboy philosophy."

Playboyism is, as we have seen, a brief moment in the history of the sexual revolution; it stands, anyway, under strong suspicion (like more than a few religious movements) of using high-minded doubletalk as cover for less noble objectives, such as increasing the opportunity for men to "score." But the same religiosity can be found in other leaders of the sexual revolution: gravity, self-certainty, greatly disinterested and scientific motives, outrage and disgust against the oppressive powers from which we can be freed, the constant, spiraling assumption that a mystery and a secret in our sexuality can be (must be) found out, for our liberation.

The model of the prophets

Many Christians react with horror to the sexual revolution. They refer to "filth" and moral degradation as if it were obvious that the open display of sexuality amounted to filth. Such a response does not answer: The faithful of the sexual revolution consider open sexuality something about which they can be proud, not ashamed.

We could learn from the Old Testament prophets. They were quite familiar with sex religions, but they did not condemn them for their sensuality. It was not their sexual content that offended; rather, it was the fact that they worshiped something other than the one true God. The charge brought against the Israelites who indulged in fertility religion was not that they were sensualists, but that they had deserted their true husband, Yahweh, for another lover.

How had they deserted God? Those who heard (and were annoyed by) the prophets remained a very spiritual people. They still worshiped at Yahweh's temple. What was so wrong with accepting some of the good points in other people's religion? Didn't all the world know that sex was part of fertility, and fertility was what made the crops grow, and the crops were what made life possible? Was it so wrong to honor this in a religious context?

The prophets' answer was that there is only one God to be worshiped. He has no rivals. He alone saves; he alone provides blessing and wisdom.

Sex-centered religions, ancient and modern, look elsewhere for blessing. They look to powerful forces—the power of pleasure, of fertility, of maleness and femaleness, of ecstasy. Whether or not these forces are related overtly to gods, they gain a divine status. One seeks to release their power in one's life.

Ancient Israel, by contrast, was not called to study power. Israelites were not noted for their technology (they were less sophisticated than their neighbors), their politics, or their magic. Elijah's contest with the prophets of Baal was impressive, but exceptional—and there is no record of the Israelites ever thinking of duplicating it. (They could not duplicate it. Only God could—and he did not.) Israelites were always a weak people who relied on the power found through loyal personal relationships: to one another in their family, tribal, and national covenants, and primarily to a personal God in whose image they were made. Power was of secondary significance. If they were faithful to God, he would provide what they needed.

The Bible is manifestly not against sex or sensuality. Both are understood throughout as part of God's good creation, made to be enjoyed. But the faithful Israelite's first question about sex was not how to gain power or happiness from it, but how sexuality should reflect faith in God.

On this basis, before all others, Christians must evaluate the sexual revolution. To the extent that it is an assertion of human potential apart from God, it is wrong.

After twenty years of marriage, Rita's husband, Jack, brought home a sex manual. Rita found it, and with hardly a second glance threw it in the trash.

Jack asked, "What did you do that for?"

"I'm not going to have pornography in my home," Rita answered, in a matter-of-fact voice that Jack knew well.

"That's not pornography," Jack said. "It was written by a doctor. For heaven's sake, I just thought it might help us."

"What's wrong with us?" Rita asked.

Jack gathered his courage. "I didn't say anything was wrong with us, honey. I just thought we could be enjoying our sex life more."

"I don't know how anybody could enjoy it more than you already do," Rita said, rather curtly. "I have never, in all these years, said no to you. Never."

Thus far I have tried to put the sexual revolution into context as a quasi-religious movement. Now I want to look more closely at what the sexual revolution rebelled against. How did it come to be that sex and sensuality were treated as such dangers, but hardly ever as joys? Why did the Old Consensus teach someone like Rita to think of a sex manual as pornography?

In the religious traditions of the East, sex manuals—like the one Rita threw in the trash—would have seemed fairly ordinary. Similar works (notably India's *Kama Sutra*) have flourished since at least the third or fourth century A.D. They were not regarded as indecent or obscene; a bride might expect one as a gift for her wedding. They discussed an ingenious diversity of sexual positions, along with questions of timing, caressing, kissing, biting, and scratching. Islam, Buddhism, and Confucianism all adopted versions of these books. But the West did not.

At about the time in which the *Kama Sutra* was composed, the Roman emperor Constantine—whose subjects would not necessarily have gone to India for lessons in the erotic arts—was turning his empire toward official Christianity. The *Kama Sutra* was not to enter the West, for the Christian West took a course that would not tolerate it.

It is a puzzle to many how a civilization that knew all the pleasures of unbridled sexuality could turn toward Christianity, which has been widely vilified as antisexual. Some have described Christianity as the most antisexual religion ever. They are mistaken, both because there are genuinely antisexual religions—notably, the oldest forms of Buddhism—and because the Christian mainstream never went so far as to brand sex as evil. Any time sex was identified as evil—as it sometimes was in the early centuries, by gnostics or Manichaeans—that view was identified as heresy. Sex was too clearly part of God's good creation to be called bad.

A negative stance toward sex
From very early on, though, many Christian leaders took a negative stance toward sex. They had two reasons. One was their belief that

celibacy was a higher calling than marriage. If celibacy was best, it followed that anyone who married was a second-rate Christian. Celibacy certainly had a great significance for much of Western history, and later in this book I will discuss it in more detail.

The Christian leaders' other concern is easier for us to understand today. Christians of the Roman Empire thought of sex as a danger, and they identified the danger—Augustine, in particular, made this identification—as losing control. That is why Augustine thought sex was always on the edge of sinfulness: its passion was irrational.

I say that this is easier for us to understand because I believe we remain at least unsettled by our spontaneous sexual responses. I think of a small boy whose parents discovered him covering his penis with his hand while he watched TV. His parents asked him why he was doing that, and he explained that "it pops up when it sees a girl." He felt his sexuality was distinct from himself; it acted on its own. For Augustine, this was at the opposite pole from freedom; it made man a slave to tyrannical passions.

Indeed, passion can present a frightening side. Consider a truly great, courageous, and self-controlled Christian: Martin Luther King, Jr. We know now that infidelity filled him with self-loathing and depression, and that he desperately feared being exposed by the FBI. He jeopardized, time and again, the cause he lived and died for in the name of Christ. Why? Or fill in some other less-public name—some ex-pastor who is now selling insurance. Could Satan have offered any other temptation (a million dollars tax-free, or a guest appearance on the "Tonight" show) to make him forfeit his calling, his wife, and his children?

Leaders are not the only ones so cursed by irrationality. Usually, when we hear that some friend or relative has deserted spouse and children, we are stunned less by the evil of the deed than by the implausibility. "What on Earth could make her do it?" we want to know.

It is a terrible sadness: We must guard ourselves in the very realm that calls us to self-abandonment and euphoria. Augustine described this sick contradiction: "For though [the passions] are regulated by a bridling and restraining power, which those who live temperately, justly, and godly exercise, sometimes with ease, and sometimes with greater difficulty, this is not the sound health of nature, but the weakness which results from sin."

Augustine's freedom

Oddly enough, embedded in Augustine's pessimistic assessment of sex is the idea of freedom. For Augustine passionately believed in freedom, including sexual freedom.

Augustine's idea of God's perfect creation was not a world in which everyone followed orders, but a world in which human beings were completely, joyfully free to do what they wanted—and knew what they wanted was wholly good. For Augustine, the tragic effect of the Fall was that, left to ourselves, we can no longer do exactly what we want. Fallen man's mind and his body do not obey his will. "For in spite of himself his mind is both frequently disturbed, and his flesh suffers, and grows old, and dies; and in spite of ourselves we suffer whatever else we suffer, and which we would not suffer if our nature absolutely and in all its parts obeyed our will." The fact that we must guard ourselves, and even do battle with ourselves, marks our loss of radical freedom. Nowhere is this more evident to Augustine than in our sexual conduct, where even our organs embarrass us by disregarding our will.

Augustine's solution was to try to rule passion out of sex—or at least to limit it. But, of course, the church fathers knew as well as we do that passionless sex is all but a contradiction in terms. So they had a skittish view of sex: necessary, at least potentially good, but invariably troublesome and dangerous.

Later, beginning with Aquinas, theologians allowed room for passion between married partners, so long as the principal, "rational" reasons for sex—procreation, particularly—were maintained. Passion was not always evil, but it remained suspect, a source of danger.

The theologians' insistence that sex behave rationally—that is, that it lead to its supposedly proper purpose of children—led to strange twists. Aquinas, for instance, considered masturbation worse than rape, since rape might still lead to the proper end of procreation.

People who emphasized the dangers of sex were all too apt to slip into thinking of the body itself as evil. Odilon of Cluny, writing in the eleventh century about sexual intercourse, asked, "We, who would be loath to touch vomit or dung even with our fingertip—how can we desire to clasp in our arms the bag of excrement itself?" One cannot be further from the attitudes of Eden, where Adam and Eve were "one flesh," naked and unashamed. Odilon is closer to the attitude taught in the Buddhist scriptures, where a monk was to contemplate the human body like a butcher displaying a cow's carcass; he should think of it "encased in skin and full of various impurities: nails, skin, teeth . . . stomach, excrement, bile, phlegm, pus, blood, sweat, tears."

To confront the dangers of sexual passion, medieval Christianity developed detailed manuals that priests used in taking confession. Some manuals instructed priests to delve into the most minute detail of a person's sexual life, including the frequency, positions, and sensations of intercourse. The priest, representing God, was to supervise the most intimate relations of married life. (A modern therapist might ask similar questions and wield similar authority for a similar reason—to make sex serve the good. But there is this important difference: therapy is voluntary, while confession was not.)

The Reformation and beyond

The Reformation changed Protestant Europe's view of sexuality. Marriage, which had been second-rate and unspiritual, became the norm almost overnight. Luther considered celibacy virtually impossible for most men, and certainly not a way that led anyone closer to heaven. Perhaps more than Luther's theorizing, his example—a turbulent yet happy marriage after a lifetime of celibacy—had a very great impact. The Reformation also put an end to priestly confession, and in a practical sense freed people's sexual lives from the church. Since the Bible said nothing about positions, frequencies, and sensations, Protestant ministers did not either. What married people did in their bed was a matter to be settled with God, not the pastor.

Yet the Reformation retained the suspicion of passion. Luther's ambivalence shows clearly in his concluding sentence to *The Estate of Marriage:* "Intercourse is never without sin; but God excuses it by his grace because the estate of marriage is his work, and he preserves in and through the sin all that good which he has implanted and blessed in marriage." Sex remained a danger, a danger that marriage contained, and to some degree transformed.

The Puritans, despite their reputation, were relatively positive about sexuality, for they had a warm understanding of the value of family life. Yet even for them, and much more as the interest in sexuality increased during the Victorian age, the subject of sexuality remained hemmed in by caution. It is still so for many Christians. They have an immediate seizure of conservatism when sex is mentioned. They are rule oriented. (Consider the nearly endless discussions of the morality of petting.) "Life, the puritan argues, may not be quite as much fun if you accept his perspective, but it's a lot safer," writes Andrew Greeley. So the Old Consensus has taught us.

What's inside the boundaries?

Ironically, during the same time when the West was throwing the Old Consensus out, the rest of the world was adopting it. Now, when you visit almost any country of the Two-thirds World—whether India, Iraq, China, Ghana—you will find that Puritanism has taken root. Until recently, Indian movies could not show couples kissing—in India, land where temples are decorated with copulating couples! These non-Western nations typically envy the West its technology, but fear and scorn its sexual morality. They prefer the morality of the Victorians. From a global perspective, it is not clear that the Old Consensus is finished.

But as the West has turned its hope more and more to sex, caution has seemed less and less adequate. The boundaries and dangers may be well defined, but what will happen within the boundaries? The question has changed from *When is sex legitimate?* to *When is sex good?* Sex, modern people will say, is all about pleasure and intimacy—not caution. In fact, caution interferes with pleasure and intimacy. Our time recognizes no gargoyle more ghastly than the uptight, repressed male who is out of touch with his feelings.

Sex is a passionate activity, a joy, and a fascination. Yet what has the Western Christian tradition said about this? Essentially: "Stay within the lines," and, "Watch yourself." The Old Consensus said next to nothing about delight, joy, comfort, and ecstasy.

If in our time many search for a return to a sexual Eden, perhaps it is partly because the Old Consensus wrote a sexual Eden completely off the map.

Chapter 3

THE NEW
SALVATION

*W*hat we need is a new morality freeing sex from the old anxieties, the old inhibitions, and from the social and sexual supremacy of one sex over the other, all of which are damaging to the full enjoyment of sex for both females and males. A new sexual ethic will have to be as definite as was the old one; but it ought to be a morality flowing from man's inner values, not one imposed on him by authority or tradition. . . .

In short, it will have to be a sexual morality which results in a secure bond, free of any bondage. It will have to be a morality that facilitates sexual, emotional and social relationships in which each partner finds deep satisfaction of his dependent needs; but within which he can also afford to develop his individuality to the fullest, due to the pleasure each partner finds in watching the other achieve his self-realization. Such self-realization will be more readily available because each sexual partner will know that whatever weaknesses may come in the wake of his greater strengths will not be taken advantage of, but will be compensated for with loving care. Such a new morality will permit sexual relations to be fully satisfying in both their active and their passive aspects; strength in the partner will be admired without being

resented; dependent needs of the partner will not be taken advantage of,
but experienced as an opportunity to deepen the bond and to enrich the
relation.

—Bruno Bettelheim, "About the Sexual Revolution"

Bruno Bettelheim is far from an excitable radical. He is the very
essence of a calm, cultured, controlled psychoanalyst. Yet there is a
strong scent of utopia in these paragraphs, as in much that is written
about sexuality these days.

Two qualities stand out. One is optimism. Bettelheim is not
describing a set of unrealizable ideals; he is describing a situation
that he apparently expects to see, or at least expects his children to
see. He uses the future tense ("such a new morality will permit
sexual relations to be fully satisfying") rather than conditional
("such a new morality would permit sexual relations to be fully
satisfying"). In theological terms, he has an imminent eschatology:
The kingdom of heaven is just ahead.

The second noteworthy quality is the lack of respect for tradition.
"It ought to be a morality flowing from man's inner values, not one
imposed on him by authority or tradition. . . ." Bettelheim takes for
granted the difference between authority and tradition, on the one
hand, and man's inner values, on the other. But as G. K. Chesterton
argued, authority and tradition *do* flow from man's inner values;
where else could they possibly come from? Tradition is democracy
extended in time, Chesterton said. Tradition brings us the ideas not
merely of those currently walking around, but also of those who are
dead. By this, tradition preserves us from the tyranny of the Latest
Idea. For Bettelheim, however, the dead are rejected. They have
nothing to tell us about our inner values, for we are the New Men
and Women.

These two points are characteristic of many modern writings
about sexuality. They promise salvation here and now—a heaven on
Earth such as has never existed in the history of the Earth. They
expect this salvation to be invented by our generation, acting on its
own inner values rather than any traditional understanding. Some
might look to India or ancient China for insight, but far more often
they look to Masters and Johnson. It would not be quite accurate to
say that sex is to be our salvation. Rather, we are to be our own
saviors, drawing up our code of conduct and belief, and centering

our quest for salvation in the region of sexuality—in sexual pleasure, in relationships providing "a secure bond, without any bondage," in maleness and femaleness that will want and do only the best for each other.

The modern, secular version of sexual salvation has a loosely defined set of substitutions for traditional religious categories:
- for heaven, we substitute pleasure (or intimacy);
- for finding God, we substitute finding yourself;
- for forgiveness of sins, we substitute forgetting;
- for the Ten Commandments, we substitute therapeutic values;
- for good works, we substitute good intentions;
- for Scripture, we substitute science.

For heaven, we substitute pleasure (or intimacy). That is simply to say that pleasure is what we think we were made for, what we long to experience, and what we work and suffer for.

Irene Kassorla's *Nice Girls Do,* which spent 22 weeks on the *New York Times* best-seller list, offers hard-sell evangelism for this gospel: "How many of you have experienced the optimum in sexuality: *complete* emotional and physical satiation? And how many among you have ever heard of an orgasm called the 'maxi'? Few women in the world have."

She continues, "You're the only one who can make it happen *for you.*

"You deserve the pleasure.

"You deserve to be a *happy, fulfilled* woman.

"... Every nerve ending can become sensitized to the sensual experience: your shoulders, your cheeks, your fingers, your toes— everything! You'll be able to orgasm as easily with someone touching your back as you will when someone touches your clitoris. And afterwards you will revel in complete contentment and peace with yourself—feeling energetic and refueled, ready to tackle a busy schedule at work or at home.

"... Every woman reading this book can learn how to make her sexual hopes and fantasies become living realities. You can stop comparing yourself negatively with other women; you don't need to feel different or inadequate anymore. You can be the exciting, sensual woman you've envied in books and seen in films."

Having described heaven, Kassorla gives her definition of trage-

dy. "The tragedy of most sex is that it ends with the first orgasm."
Very often good sex is described in the language of the gourmet.
Dr. Ruth writes, "I believe in educating people to be sexual gourmets. This is a very simple idea. In everyday life we talk a lot about
food and diets. We exchange recipes and introduce one another to
different cuisines and culinary techniques. We are happy to share
the discoveries we have made in the kitchen. So why shouldn't we
feel just as comfortable exchanging recipes for better sexual
functioning?"

The gourmet must try new recipes, and the sexual gourmet must
vary his or her sexual techniques. The lowest form of sexuality is the
missionary position, not because it is a bad position, but because
couples may get "stuck" there and not try other approaches. For
some it follows that new partners increase the pleasure as well.

Others would claim that the best gourmet sex is possible only in
marriage. Sex therapist Paul Pearsall, director of education for the
Kinsey Institute, asserts that "Super marital sex is the most erotic,
intense, fulfilling experience any human being can have. Anony-
mous sex with multiple partners pales by comparison. . . . No form
of extramarital sex can compete with super marital sex, and once
this lesson is learned, spouses having affairs may begin cheating on
their 'lovers,' and having 'intramarital' sex with their husband or
wife." Josh McDowell, whose Christian seminars on "Maximum
Sex" have attracted huge college audiences, presumably agrees.

How would Hugh Hefner respond to such assertions? Probably by
claiming that Paul Pearsall and Josh McDowell know little about the
pleasure found in the Playboy mansions, and certainly by asserting
that every man and woman is free to search for pleasure in the way
that suits him or her best. (Isn't there something in the Declaration
of Independence about that?) When pleasure is the object, who can
judge another?

But in truth, as we have seen, most people lose interest in a Hugh
Hefner–type search for pleasure. The quest for intimacy, which
takes its place, suggests something different from pleasure seeking.

But just what is intimacy? The bare word suggests people who
know each other deeply, whose lives are intertwined. But intimacy
does not always work out that way. Sometimes intimacy happens
between people who have just met. On the other hand, intimacy may
grow stale after half a lifetime together. Intimacy cannot be defined

by objective criteria, for it is a state of the feelings.

Intimacy, I would suggest, amounts to another kind of pleasure—the pleasure found in a person (as distinct from a body). It is broader and deeper than the pleasure Irene Kassorla describes—it offers emotional and intellectual as well as sensuous intensity—but it is still pleasure found through sexual relations. As such, it can only be defined by the person experiencing it. He or she alone knows what feels good.

It seems increasingly obvious that the pathway to sexual pleasure is not straight. Therapist Alexander Lowen notes, "There is available to the public an extensive literature that describes the sexual techniques of different cultures, East and West. Unfortunately, it offers no insight or help for the problems of sexual unhappiness that are presented daily to physicians, psychiatrists, and marriage counselors." Sex therapists deal increasingly with people who, despite great sexual sophistication, find little pleasure in sex.

Lowen goes on to ask, "If a person finds that he has no desire for food, he would hardly describe his lack of appetite as a failure. If this is not a failure, why is the loss of sexual desire so regarded?" The answer is obvious: Those who don't thoroughly enjoy sex believe that something important is missing from their lives. A Christian who had lost his desire to pray might feel a similar emptiness—though only if he were an unusually committed believer. In sex, we have no shortage of committed believers. They believe that they were made for intense sexual pleasure. Lacking such pleasure, they are sure they are headed for hell.

For finding God, we substitute finding yourself. In traditional Christianity, heaven is where God is. The joy of his presence defines the joy of heaven. Thus, whenever someone experiences God, it can be said that he experiences the kingdom of heaven.

Modern sexual salvation offers no God, or considers him a peripheral figure. So what does a person find in the heaven of pleasure? He finds himself.

What does it mean to find yourself? Old definitions of Homo sapiens as a thinking creature, or as a moral creature, seem out of date. You do not find such creatures when you find yourself. You find a feeling creature, "in touch with his feelings," aware of his own drives and able to express them freely. Of course, sexual pleasure is the apex of feeling. Therefore, it offers the key opportunity for finding yourself, the feeling creature.

The feeling creature is able to let go, to relax, to stop worrying about performing. He responds to the moment. His caring for others never interferes with his primary allegiance to his own feeling. In *Intimacy: The Essence of Male and Female,* Shirley Luthman puts it this way: "Maximum growth for the individual is dependent on his capacity to express who he is—*which means his feelings*—clearly, congruently, and spontaneously" (italics added).

A happy relationship, as our generation conceives it, is two individuals glowing with the healthy confidence born of finding themselves. The emphasis is not on their delight in each other, but on their satisfaction with how a shared life affects their self-satisfaction.

Listen to Arlene Kagle writing in *Mademoiselle:* "Each of us naturally alternates between a desire to be close to someone and a desire to act independently, to get off on our own for a while. You might crave intimacy more often than autonomy, or perhaps you're the kind of person who more often wants solitude; in any case, the balance of these needs is a crucial part of your personality. We'll call this balance a person's intimacy/autonomy (I/A) ratio. It has everything to do with your sense of . . . 'fit' with a particular partner.

"In a good relationship . . . there is an easy flow in which closeness and distance alternate comfortably. When this equilibrium isn't present, the relationship is troubled. . . . If you can learn how to speak out of your own conflict-free space and express your needs while respecting another's you are on your way to a better relationship. . . . Rest assured, the effort will be well worth it."

Here we see the familiar emphasis on compatibility, expressed as "fit." The key to a good fit is finding yourself (knowing your own "I/A ratio," "speaking out of your own conflict-free space," "expressing your needs"). Finding yourself may lead to relationship—that is, to a comfortable fit. But clearly, that relationship does not focus on your partner's unique qualities. You respect his needs, but it is your own with which you must really interact. You want the relationship for your own satisfaction—as your partner is expected to want it for hers or his. In the world as conceived by popular psychology, each individual floats freely in the universe, feeling his or her own needs, choosing attachments (and breaking attachments) on the basis of those felt needs.

The attachments can never—your partner can never—make a strong claim on you. Only your feelings have a claim on you. Essentially, you are finding pleasure in finding yourself, and finding yourself in feeling pleasure. Others mainly provide the context. What happens when a partner betrays you? The fear of betrayal is a constant undertheme in pleasure-seeking lives. No one can guarantee that a partner will find him or her a fulfilling experience tomorrow. So intimacy is undercut by a wariness toward other people—a sense that ultimately they ought not be depended on.

For the forgiveness of sins, we substitute forgetting. Dr. Ruth is a very attractive, accepting sort of mother figure. People feel they can tell her anything without being condemned, even though she makes clear that some deeds—like unfaithfulness in a "closed" relationship—ought to be avoided. Nonetheless, one phrase rings through her advice: "It happened." As in advising a man who has cheated on his wife and consequently caught herpes: "These things do happen. For you I think the most important thing right now is not to think about regretting for the rest of your life, and not to think what you ought to have done, because it happened. I think what you ought to do is take your wife out for dinner, or a ride, and then go home [and talk]. Don't do it someplace outside, because if she does want to be angry, or cry, or whatever, she should have that freedom either in the car or at home."

Herpes made truth-telling inevitable in this particular case; the man's lesions were so obvious he could not even undress in front of his wife. When unpleasant truth telling can be avoided, however, Dr. Ruth thinks you should. "It happened" means, let's try to overlook it, if we can. If not, let's talk about it. Either way, let's go on from here without dwelling on the past any more than is strictly necessary.

Sexual mistrust and betrayal make deep wounds. The sexual revolution offers no way to deal with these wounds, except by "working them through" therapeutically, and trying to forget.

For the Ten Commandments, we substitute therapeutic values. The values that guide a therapist include: to accept people as they are, to be sympathetic as you help them understand and accept themselves, to assist them in making their own choices. These are quite distinct from more traditional values that clergy were once known for: to teach people to want to be right, inwardly and outwardly; to help them to measure themselves against God's standards; to foster the choice to love and obey God, and to discourage any other choice. The moralist is a surgeon, cutting away cancerous tissue. The therapist is a midwife, optimistically assuming that amid the chaos of any life something is being born, something that only needs assistance.

The therapist's tolerance, acceptance, and patience can be a great relief to wounded and wounding people. But removed from any moral context, the therapist would not be really kind, and his acceptance would not be a relief. If nothing is right and nothing is wrong, why not be accepting? It would be irrational and cruel not to be. In reality, though, the therapist's work is never really isolated from a moral context. The therapist sits in an office, alone with a client, yet is well aware of society outside. A family, a spouse, an organization, or a business demands certain standards of behavior; the therapist provides a 50-minute refuge from society's judgments in order to explore the reasons behind and the possibilities of escape from whatever is making his client unhappy.

When the therapist's office grows to consume the whole world, though, we enter a very different situation. James B. Nelson, perhaps the best-known liberal theologian of sex, writes, "God's radical, unconditional, and unearned acceptance of us is a fitting contemporary translation of justification by grace." If so, that acceptance is not the same as the therapist's. The therapist chooses not to judge behavior that he would surely have to judge if it occurred in his home; he suspends judgment. If his client tells him that he kills and eats neighborhood dogs, the therapist covers his shock and mildly says, "How do you feel about that?" He does the same if his client tells him that he slept with fifteen women last week. God's acceptance is quite different: based not on willed amnesia, but on mercy. His judgment is not suspended, but absorbed at great personal cost in the death of his dear Son. The sin is confronted in all its deadly power, so that while the accepted sinner escapes that power, he knows even while being accepted that what he has done is tragic and deadly.

Nelson further writes, "If it be argued that we can reject the sin without rejecting the sinner, the question must be asked, but what if the so-called 'sin' is as much a part of the person as the color of the skin?" To this question we must rejoin: What other kind of sin is there? Sins are not clothes that we put on or take off. Sin sinks its roots into the heart, and we sinners are powerless to dig them out.

Righteous acceptance of sinners is grounded only in the agonizing death for sin of Jesus. This is quite at odds with contemporary attitudes, according to which sins (if they exist at all) call not for death, but for a therapeutic pat on the back and a word of pseudo-grace: "That's okay."

For good works, we substitute good intentions. Orthodox Christianity regards good deeds as essential. God's grace always seeks a visible response. Those being saved will act in certain ways.

This is a very material way of seeing life. The spiritual realm must demonstrate its reality in the physical realm. But our secular society, while acknowledging the power of good deeds (it admires Mother Teresa), finds it increasingly hard to specify any behavior as required. Good works are negotiable; what is nonnegotiable is that you be a "good person."

A best-selling book made this quality explicit in its title: *When Bad Things Happen to Good People*. The title apparently made instant sense to millions: in modern minds, there is a category of "good people" who do not deserve to have bad things happen to them. Every bad thing they receive is an injustice.

But who are these good people? Are they saints? Perhaps they are in Rabbi Kushner's thinking, but I daresay most of his readers thought of good people as "people like me." They don't do anything bad enough to make the six o'clock news. Even when they cause harm or hurt others, they really do not intend to. They have good intentions. So they don't deserve to have bad things happen to them.

Are there "bad people" who *do* deserve to have bad things happen to them? Maybe a few: murderers, rapists, racists, child molesters. Rarely do they live in our neighborhood. Certainly they are not *us*.

Then why is it that so many relationships between "good people" seethe with anger and pain? Both mean well; they never intended to hurt each other. So why are gaping wounds apparent—not only in the couple, but in their family members? Why is our neighborhood, so full of good people, also full of broken families and divorces and abortions and—you name it? Why, when Charles Kuralt can find good people everywhere, is the world in such a mess?

Our society turns out to be, not materialistic as sometimes charged, but spiritualistic. "Good people" are those whose spirits are good. But there is no necessary connection between good people and good deeds, between good people and intact families, between good people and happy relationships. Things "just happen." In sexual matters particularly, our generation is unable to think seriously about the consequences of acts done by the body.

One could cite many examples. The consequences of divorce on children, of promiscuity on the growth of poverty, of sex-saturated television on teenage pregnancies—all are briefly looked at, then passed over. The most penetrating recent example has been the inability of modern moralists to grasp the implications of AIDS.

When international conferences on AIDS are held, it would be considered terribly bad form to emphasize that the disease could never sustain an epidemic without behavior traditionally considered immoral. Experts concentrate entirely on controlling the effects of the disease—through condoms, through vaccines. No one wants to say that the AIDS epidemic is at least partly caused and perpetuated by sexual promiscuity. That would seem, in that classic phrase of no-fault modernity, to "blame the victim." Can anyone doubt that these victims are "good people"?

James Nelson published his thoughts on "Responding to, Learning from AIDS" in *Christianity and Crisis*. All he appears to have learned from AIDS is that homophobic responses have made coping with the epidemic more difficult. His interest is not in the (bodily) disease at all, or how people get it, but in the reaction of people who don't have it. Nelson is an interesting case of the spiritualism of modernism. He is noted for emphasizing the unity of mind and body (his best-known book is titled *Embodiment*), but he appears not to grasp that one inevitable aspect of being a body is that actions often have consequences. He writes of sex as a "language" capable of expressing many different meanings through a limited repertoire of actions. In other words, it is not what you do so much as what you intend by it. There is some truth to that, but not the whole truth. What ordinary people have learned from AIDS is that sex is not merely a way of expressing feelings; it is a physical act with physical consequences. Those consequences are capable of killing you, in some cases. I hesitate to call AIDS the judgment of God. I do suspect it to be the judgment of nature on a theory of sex without consequences.

For Scripture, we substitute science. Before the Enlightenment, Western people believed that God was intimately involved with every feature of life, public as well as private. Since then, God has been eliminated from public life: government, economics, education. He is being pushed out of private life, too. Sex has lost a sense of God's concern. It is simply a way for two people to be together. While people once thought the Bible revealed the truth about their lives, they now look to science for revelation. Sex can be analyzed and explained through laboratory experiments like those Masters and Johnson undertook, or through questionnaires like Kinsey's. If Scripture were considered at all, its truthfulness would be examined by asking whether it agreed with scientific findings.

The scientific approach tends to make sex more a "thing" that can be broken down into its components, manipulated, even altered. The atom has been conquered; why not sex? This way of harnessing its power would be impossible, however, if sex were concealed in modest silences. Science requires full disclosure. Kinsey needed people who would answer personal questions. Masters and Johnson needed people who would copulate in the laboratory. And neither they nor their successors could do their work without a society that gave them grants, bought their books, invited them to talk on TV. Ironically, during the same period that sex became viewed as a strictly private matter, it also began to dominate social discourse.

In earlier times, a person could go through the day without seeing or hearing any mention of sex, unless it was from his spouse or from some friends of the same sex. Today any one of us encounters sexual stimulation many times a day, often from someone whose very existence is the figment of an advertising director's imagination. We live in a constant bath of depersonalized, imaginary, highly provocative sexuality. To the modern person, this seems normal; he is barely aware of it.

This climate is sometimes abused, most people admit—by pornographers, for instance. There is no changing it, though. A climate of complete sexual candor is essential if we are to understand sex through science. Additionally, our openly sexual environment offers many more opportunities to explore our sexual feelings, and thus find ourselves.

Joanne is a tiny, striking brunette who heads data control for a large food distributor. She took several years to accept her divorce, for she had really loved Nate. They reunited several times before giving it up for good.

Now she is quite cynical about the conservative sexual ethics she grew up with. "It's hard to believe I swallowed that whole line," she says to her friend Ruth, who has met her for coffee. "When I think of the energy I put into saving my virginity, it stupefies me."

For two years now, Joanne and Hank have been together. Once, when he developed a stomach ulcer, she moved in with him, but feeling not quite right she went back to her own apartment when he recovered. Hank teaches ethics in a business school, and he is sometimes quoted in Newsweek. Everybody likes him, and Joanne feels fortunate to have him. Or almost to have him.

One weekend Hank didn't answer the phone; he admitted later, after only a little resistance, that he had been with his former wife. He didn't offer any apologies, and Joanne felt she couldn't make a scene—she didn't own him. It turned out not to be too rare an event. Once he took a working associate to ski in Switzerland for a week.

"I guess it bothers me," Joanne confesses to Ruth, "because my biological clock is ticking. Oh, maybe I am a little jealous, but I can live with it. However, I would like to have kids, and I think Hank would make a wonderful father. I just don't feel settled. I certainly don't feel solid enough to go ahead and have a child. Do you think that's just an excuse? I mean, do you think my upbringing is getting through to me?"

What does Joanne really want? A conventional hubby and a house in the suburbs? A child? A closer relationship? An exclusive hold on Hank? What do any of us want? Our desires are broad and ill-defined. Rarely do we know exactly what we want until we are given a specific set of choices. In modern America, the choices are very wide. Yet for Joanne, or for anyone, the implications of the choices are very deep.

Focus on Joanne, and you will see how great a difference our theology of sexual salvation makes. The Old Consensus told her one thing, which still hangs in the back of her mind. The new sexual salvation, which she has absorbed from magazines and TV and best-selling books, tells her something quite different.

It tells her to look to her sexuality—her sexual pleasure, her intimacy with Hank—for the focus of meaning in life. Through these pleasures she can find herself, learning not to deny her feelings.

It tells her she has no claim on Hank. She can only express her feelings. If those feelings go with Hank's feelings, they will continue together. If not, they will move on.

It tells her that compatibility is the foundation of her relationship to Hank. Apparently they fit. Or do they? Possibly her restlessness derives from some feelings that she is not in touch with. Joanne needs to explore these feelings, to know whether she and Hank really are compatible. (If they're not, it's best to end things quickly. You can't change yourself to please a man, and it would be wrong to try to change him.)

It tells her to remain resolutely disinterested in what went wrong in her marriage. "It happened."

It tells her to reject brusquely anyone who suggests that her relational arrangement with Hank is wrong. She will not be dominated by an outdated morality. How she lives is her business, no one else's, and only she can know what is right for her.

The challenge

This modern code is posing a challenge—a severe one—to Christian thinking about sex. I don't consider the challenge all bad. Christian thinking has been badly inadequate. Its negativism was unbiblical, and its concern for control made a dominant feature out of something that, scripturally, is secondary. Its acceptance of the double standard was immoral. Worst of all, it had nothing very positive to say. Eden had been forgotten.

The challenge has already changed the way in which Christians talk about sexuality. Church seminars today can be quite explicit and idealistic about sex, in a way that seemed impossible a short time ago. Yet this new idealism often seems to mimic secular optimism. It seems to accept Hugh Hefner's challenge. Imagine:

Hefner: "Why are you Christians so uptight about people getting a little pleasure?"

Seminar leader: "We're not. Frankly, we're all for pleasure. Our God is a God of pleasure. The Bible says he made all things for us to enjoy. The fact is, a Christian marriage has the potential for sexual pleasure like you never heard of."

Which may be true. The trouble is, in accepting Hefner's challenge we seem also to accept Hefner's premise: that pleasure is the ultimate aim of sex. I am not certain that Christians would win a contest of hedonism, and I am certain they should not want to enter one. It is not possible to accept the premises of a secular salvation, and then add on God as an afterthought.

We need a resorting, both of the Old Consensus, and of the sexual revolution. In each, there is good as well as harm. In each, there are powerful ideals that may be twisted into something powerfully destructive.

We need a pragmatic resorting, but we also need a religious resorting. The Old Testament prophets, I have suggested, are a model. Their persistent condemnation of fertility religions was not over their sensuality, though sanctified prostitution must have been horrifying to conservative Israelites. Nor was the prophets' critique pragmatic—that the crops didn't really grow any better when you fornicated in the hill shrines. Their critique was centered on the contention that there is only one God, Yahweh. Isaiah made that point well enough in scornfully describing how idols were made from a log of wood and then tacked down to the floor so they wouldn't fall over. Such a "god" is no God. There is only one God, only one who created the world, only one who gave us our sexuality. He alone deserves worship. He alone can rightly demand total allegiance. He alone can save.

To understand the biblical view of sexuality, you must ask what sex has to do with salvation—the salvation that has been revealed to Abraham, to Moses, to David, and finally revealed in and through Jesus Christ.

Chapter 4

SEX IN
AND AFTER EDEN

*I*f I understand what the Bible says about sex," my friend Ruth
*says, "I'd sum it up by saying that sex is meant to be connected.
It's not supposed to be isolated from the rest of life; it's a part of, an
expression of, the connection between, two people. And marriage is the
ultimate connection. But if that's so, why are so few Christians sexually
happy? Why doesn't the reality I see match the theory?*

*"Every marriage that I'm close to is, under the surface, unhappy. In
every one, both the husband and wife would say in their most honest
moments that they would be happier married to someone else."*

*Ruth doesn't insist that the marriages she knows are altogether
typical. She lives in a sophisticated college town. Maybe marriages in
college towns are having unusual troubles. Her own marriage is a
struggle. Perhaps she sees others' marriages through personal gloom.*

*She does insist, however, that the marriages she is talking about are
real—and that we need to take account of them in our theorizing about
how wonderful marriage is.*

Marriage is very near the heart of a Christian view of sex, so the truth
of Ruth's observations is quite crucial. It is all very well to speak

eloquently about the beauty of marriage. But just how beautiful are marriages in real life?

When I think about the marriages *I* know, I come up with a different view from Ruth's. I don't think many of my friends would say, except on a particularly bad night, that they wish they were married to someone else. But that does not mean they would readily describe their marriages as happy.

Happy? When so much time and energy goes into learning to live with each other? When so many nights one or the other of them is depressed, or angry, or uncommunicative? When the same problems that surfaced last year surface this year? A lot of married people I know are still grieving for their dying dreams. I would not describe most of their marriages as bad. But I would describe them as hard.

Happy? It is hard to be happy when one partner craves conversation and emotion, and the other prefers solitude. How did two people so unlike in personality ever fall in love?

Happy? It is hard to be happy when one partner runs up credit card bills without a shred of worry, while the other is a worrier who loses sleep every time he sees the VISA bill.

Happy? It is hard to be happy when one partner is depressed and agitated at least one day out of three, and keeps her husband awake by thrashing around in their double bed all night while grieving over lost youth or fading dreams or something—she usually only gets more agitated if you probe.

These are among the marriages I know well enough to have an idea what goes on under the surface. They are, in fact, from my list of "good" marriages. They are fine people who really do love each other. They don't have what you would call "serious problems" from the three Big A's of adultery, alcoholism, or abuse. None of them, so far as I know, suffers from deep sexual inhibitions or dysfunctions. These are not what I would call "bad" marriages. They are merely hard.

Happy and hard marriages

By contrast, "happy" comes quickly to mind in describing my own marriage. Compared to most marriages I know, mine is easy. (I know others that are equally easy—a few.) Of course, I "work at it," but the work is rarely burdensome.

I suffer few illusions that this is to my credit. My wife, Popie, and I share most of the same values, we like the same movies, we nearly always have the same reaction to people we meet. We are, in a word, compatible. We grew up in strong, loving families, and I am sure that our parents' patterns rubbed off on us. It is not hard to share life with someone you like as well as we like each other. During a few rough patches, I have realized how slight a change in our makeup or our circumstances would make a "hard" marriage in place of our easy one. But our rough patches have never stayed rough for long.

For many people, rough is all there is. Such marriages require compromise and sacrifice. A wife must, perhaps, endure her husband's moving from one job to another in a seemingly endless search for job satisfaction. A husband must, perhaps, endure his wife's deep, persistent depression, in which she tastes bitterness in everything.

Most Christians, and a good many non-Christians, would say that such compromises and sacrifices are the price you pay for a greater shared happiness. Overall, the satisfaction of married life makes it worth "working at"—even when the work is hard.

But how hard? There is a wide spectrum of troubles, from chronic messiness to chronic abusiveness. Just where does "hard" turn to "hopeless"? At what point do you say, "No more"?

When to cry "Too much"
People's answers to that depends a great deal on where they think happiness comes from. Much of our society puts its stress on happiness gained through individual freedom, and therefore has an easy conscience about separation and divorce. If someone leaves a relationship but gains greater peace of mind in doing so, well and good. (There are regretful backward glances at the cost children must pay, but rarely the suggestion that an unhappy marriage should be preserved just for them.)

Conservative Christians, on the other hand, generally put their stress on happiness gained through relationship. Every enduring relationship requires commitment, and with that goes some sacrifice of individual freedom. Christians tend to think those sacrifices are worth it.

Nonetheless, I believe most American Christians agree with our society that happiness is the reason for marriage, and thus, the ultimate reason why sacrifices are worthwhile. We might differ from non-Christians in our assessment of the chances of happiness, or the path to achieve it, but our fundamental values don't really differ. If a marriage has no realistic chance of happiness no matter how long and well people tough it out, we wonder why it should be preserved. Maybe it should—we know what Jesus thought of divorce—but most Christians I know aren't very clear on why.

That leaves us with the problem of those hard marriages. Some of them, no doubt, will get through long, rough periods and become happy. But how many? Will they all become truly happy? Or to put the question more precisely, is their state the happiest they are likely to achieve, married, unmarried, or married to different partners?

I think of my friend Paul. He was divorced from his first wife ten years ago. Both were Christians, but they had been basically unhappy from the very beginning. Eventually they gave up. Paul has remarried to a wonderful, giving person who understands his idiosyncrasies and knows how to live with him and love him. She, too, had been divorced. Now, together, they both seem very happy.

Most of us can think of people like that. Not that divorce and remarriage always have such positive effects. But they certainly do sometimes, and that has to cast doubt into the minds of all those who are struggling with hard marriages. Do they really need to struggle?

Push far enough along on the spectrum of troubles, and very few people would insist that every marriage be kept intact. Infidelity, drug addiction, mental illness, physical or sexual abuse, frigidity, homosexuality, long-term unemployment: as these and other severe problems persist over years, an increasing number of people would stop insisting on sacrifice. At some point the question becomes, "Sacrifice for what?" From a practical point of view, many marriages seem hopeless of ever achieving happiness.

Are Christians happier?
So what about the theory my friend Ruth referred to? It is implied in many Christian books on sex and marriage: Christians—at least Christians who follow God's directions—will be happier than others. They will feel security, love, and self-giving in their marriages. They will experience an intimacy that just would not be possible

without the committed love Christians believe in. God will teach them and help them to love each other. But is it so? Are obedient Christians really happier in their marriages or in their sexual lives? I don't know of any marriage counselor who would say yes without taking some time to think about it. Some secular counselors, tending to be hostile toward religion, would even say that Christians are the most sexually and maritally tormented of the clients they see.

I think their bias blinds them. They don't value the marriage bond all that highly, so they tend to miss its values. They value individual freedom, so they tend to overlook the misery that detached individuals create for themselves. I'd have to differ from Ruth's assessment. I would assert that the books are generally right: Christians *are*, on the average, more happily married than others.

First of all, Christian marriages tend to be loving. Every Christian is to live caringly, even when his partner doesn't deserve it. I am not saying that Christians live up to this standard—I know I don't—but at least they acknowledge that they ought to. To some extent they try. After all, Jesus gave his life for us when we least deserved it. His example, if it is followed, creates a climate of love and acceptance that can heal many wounds.

We have a hand-worked motto on our bedroom wall that says it well: "To love and be loved is the greatest joy on Earth." Quite evidently, real love must swallow faults, pain, difficulty. That may be hard, but it is also ultimately happy. Who does not want to live in that kind of gracious climate?

Second, Christian marriages tend to be secure. Divorce has certainly invaded every sector of our society, including the church, but Christians resist it. They are more likely to marry intending a strong commitment "so long as we both shall live." Such people don't have to re-evaluate their marriage's future every time they have a fight. They can put their energy, instead, into long-term solutions to their problems. To put it crassly, if they know they will have to put up with each other for the rest of their lives, they will feel freer to take some action to improve the marriage. Security breeds happiness, both because it reduces anxiety and because it frees both partners to invest wholeheartedly in their relationship.

Third, Christian marriages will tend to feel safe from disease. Just a short time ago, that seemed a negligible consideration. Today, in the era of AIDS, it begins to seem significant. Anxiety about diseases can affect a person's view, indeed a society's view, of sex. Bruno Bettelheim, writing before AIDS or herpes came into view, commented, "The Victorian attitude that sex is ugly cannot be fully understood without reference to venereal diseases. It is such an ugly and scary sickness that loathing of it extended back to the act through which it was transmitted. . . . Modern youth cannot really understand how their grandparents could have viewed sex as ugly, because they have never experienced the haunting fear of venereal infection." Now some modern youth have begun relearning that fear. But it is not necessary to do so. The plagues of AIDS, herpes, and other sexually transmitted diseases will more often be something monogamous or abstinent Christians read about in the newspaper than something they experience, or worry about, for themselves.

If any marriage is loving, secure, and safe, it will usually add a fourth quality: good sex. The couple may not match the widely advertised feats of sexual gourmets any more than the average American kitchen matches the meals displayed on TV cooking shows. But people who are committed to live caringly, who believe their marriage will last, and who are not worried about disease are likely to experience satisfying sexual relations. Well-known sex therapist Helen Singer Kaplan writes, "Sexual dysfunction is unlikely to occur in comfortable, caring relationships because there is little performance anxiety when [partners] trust and care about each other."

Of course, sexual problems can occur in very loving and secure marriages, and, on the other hand, very bad marriages can be highly erotic. A couple I know has been on the verge of divorce for years, and during all those years they have enjoyed extremely pleasurable intercourse at least once a day. But that's not common. In general, pleasurable sex is grounded in security and love.

Are Christian marriages happier? There is no precise way to measure happiness—you can only ask people how they rate themselves—but I would answer the question with a qualified yes. In general, Christians tend to have happier marriages. From a purely pragmatic point of view, the kind of marriages we support have a lot to offer the world.

The hard marriages
Yet we had better not push this too far. Neither happiness nor

marriage serve well as ends in themselves.

For one thing, we have those many "hard" marriages, and indeed, the many plainly unhappy marriages. Yes, in general Christians will tend to have happier sex lives. But what about those who do not? What are we going to say to them? That somehow they missed out on the purpose of marriage? That it's just too bad for them they don't fit what is "generally" true?

We tend to talk about marriage in unrealistically exalted terms. If marriage is supposed to be the home port of happiness, if married partners must be each other's best friends, share all of each other's interests, have ecstatic sex on a regular schedule, live in a romantic glow, and at the same time preserve the fabric of American life— well, the truth is that people who expect all this will often live, not in a continual sense of security and happiness, but in a continual state of disappointment and frustration. Most marriages won't live up to it very often. Marriage is an institution enabling two ordinary, lumpish people to share life together. Not many real people, if any, will find that heaven on Earth.

And there is another, deeper problem: These idealistic conceptions almost substitute marriage for salvation. Single people get that message quite clearly in "family-oriented" churches—they are "on hold," in perpetual adolescence until they can enter (or reenter) the fullness of life—marriage.

In our current sexual and marital confusion, it is a very tempting substitution. Many people long for security and clarity and old-fashioned values. One of the attractions of church is that it is such a family-oriented place. People would rather hear that Jesus wants to give them a happy marriage than that Jesus will forgive them for their sins.

The Mormon church has made "family orientation" central to its gospel. It has long repudiated Jesus' statement that there is no marriage in heaven, seeing (correctly) that he put marriage in a position of relative rather than absolute value. They, by contrast with Jesus, offer marriage and family life as a little piece of heaven— literally—right here on Earth. "A Parent's Guide," an official publication of the Church of Jesus Christ of Latter-day Saints, puts it this way: "Since eternal life with our Father will be lived in family units, the ultimate goal of a man or boy is to become an effective husband and father, and the ultimate goal of a woman or girl is to become an effective wife and mother." Note the use of the word *ultimate*.

The New Testament sees life very differently. The only ultimate purpose of any human being is to be the servant of Jesus Christ, whether as married or single. Jesus came into the world preaching the kingdom of God, not the family. (He warned that the kingdom would sometimes shatter families.) We know, on Jesus' authority, that our families will not carry on in heaven; something different and better will be there. The New Testament offers no grounds whatsoever for absolutizing family life. Marriage ain't heaven—nor was it meant to be.

The meaning of stories

What does the Bible tell us about our sexuality? In particular, what does it tell us about marriage? For the moment, I would like to pass over the few well-known passages in Paul's letters and Jesus' teachings. I would like to begin, not with didactic instructions, but with stories. Stories get to the heart of sex and sexuality. Yet they are often ignored or misunderstood.

Consider stories in a modern context. Consider, for example, the bodice ripper.

In the publishing business, you know a book by its cover. You certainly know bodice rippers by their covers. The woman is leaning back into the strong arms of the darkly handsome man with so much hair. Her frilled and flounced dress fits like a Brownie uniform on Dolly Parton. She is evidently having trouble breathing in the presence of this man, who looks into her eyes with cruel passion. What happens next? We all know what happens next.

In the publishing business, we would say this cover "works." It works so well that it has become a trademark, replicated again and again with minute variations. It works because you want to find out what that lusting couple will do, and how it will all turn out. You *know* how it will turn out, but millions and millions of women have paid $8.95 to find out again what they already know.

Contrast this tantalizing cover, which has sold so many millions of books, with another one that "works." It's from a recent issue of *Working Mother* magazine. There is no picture, only one big headline: "SEX VS. SLEEP: Which One Do You Pick? Be Honest."

You want to read that. At least, I do.

Unfortunately, people who buy *Working Mother* on the basis of that cover will be disappointed. What is inside is a rehash of therapists' thoughts on ISD (Inhibited Sexual Desire)—a few real-life quotes, a few statistics, and a smattering of advice. ("There's no correct sex life. You have to decide what *you* want and set your priorities for that. Communicate. Compromise. Uncover the underlying issues. If you're really troubled therapists can help you.")

I'm not faulting this stuff. However, such sane, doctor-knows-best material hardly fulfills the promise of the cover copy: "SEX VS. SLEEP: Which One Do You Pick? Be Honest."

Be honest—why do you want to read that? Because it makes you think about something not so different from what the cover of the bodice rippers makes you think about. It makes you think of a woman and a man—maybe you and yours—who want each other. But something holds them back. How will it come out? What will the couple do?

There is a story behind that cover, a story of love and desire. We get our kicks from stories, not statistics. Yet, when intelligent people start writing serious things about sex, they seem to forget all about those stories. Oh, they remember them from the publishing angle. They will include a few juicy examples to keep their readers alive. (Nowadays, all successful books on psychology or sociology describe real-life "case studies." For every bar chart you get a juicy story, sometimes two.) But in what they say about sex, those stories and our love for those stories disappear. They write about the "five critical variables of marriage," or charting your "love map." Love, sex, and marriage are somehow made as pragmatic and abstract as trade barriers between the U.S. and Canada.

Marriage as a workable compromise

This is the mindset behind an interesting piece by Warren Farrell in *Glamour* magazine, "Why Men Fear Commitment." He writes, "*Playboy* and *Penthouse* outsell all men's magazines. Why? Because they represent men's primary fantasy: access to as many beautiful women as desired without risk of rejection. Most women's primary fantasy is a relationship with one man who either provides economic security or is on his way to doing so (he has potential). For a man, commitment means giving up his primary fantasy. For a woman, commitment means fulfilling her fantasy.

". . . In the area of commitment, the man is often in the power position—to grant or deny a woman access to her primary fantasy.

But when it comes to sex, the woman is in the power seat. Yet most women want sex. And most men want to commit. So what is the underlying meaning of both sexes' nos? It is, 'You don't meet my conditions.' "

Farrell sees the world as a jungle of sexual competitors. Individuals seek to fulfill their fantasies through members of the opposite sex. When they meet someone who is "good enough"—that is, a woman who is sufficiently beautiful, or a man who makes enough money—they contract to live together. If the relationship works, and if both people are happy, it is because they both get what they wanted from the other. The man gets sex with the best-looking woman he has been able to qualify for; the woman gets commitment from the best provider she has been able to attract and hold. Thus, the institution of marriage will endure, because it is a workable compromise in male-female relations.

This is not terribly different from the way George Gilder has portrayed the sexual universe. He paints a gloomy picture of the unattached male as misanthropic, violent, unproductive, a menace to society. What is the answer for this immature gangster? Marriage! Woman, as the stable, family-oriented half of society, is able to barter her sexual privileges with a man and get him to turn his energy and violence into the productive cause of protecting and providing for his family.

I think there is more than a little truth to these pragmatic portrayals of marriage. But it is very far from the whole truth. There is no dignity for human beings in these portrayals—no altruism and little romance. All we see are individuals trying to calculate the best possible sexual deal. They marry (or don't marry) like comparison shoppers at K-Mart.

Something Dr. Ruth Westheimer wrote seemed much more true to our human situation: "I am always glad to answer . . . questions that are purely sexual. How to learn to have an orgasm, how to learn to keep an erection, what position would be best to use when people have certain difficulties during copulation, etc.

"And people love to hear these questions asked and answered on the radio, especially in the beginning, when they first listen. Because it is still startling to hear about things like adult masturbation on the radio! But when they tune in again and again (listeners have told me this) it is to hear 'the stories.' The wonderful stories of relationships that people phone in about, each story so human and yet not just like any other story."

The key word is *story*. Sex as a technical matter, as plumbing, cannot hold a person's interest for too long. Neither can sex as a kind of mathematical equation, matching the drives of one abstracted sex to another. While such abstractions of "drives" and male and female fantasies are more interesting than mere physiology, they do not capture the full interest inherent in sex. What people care about— what they will tune in to day after day are "the stories." Stories are not about classes of people. Stories are not about biology. There are no stories following a breast or a male sex drive through its adventures. Stories are about individual people, and their bonds to other people—bonds of love, anger, fear, infatuation, oppression. Stories are about how people deal with forces they discover inside themselves or around them. Stories are about persons and their growth. Stories are about the intertwining of lives. People listen to Dr. Ruth (and country-western music) for such stories.

You could interpret this to mean that sex is not nearly as interesting as people, but that would be an incorrect interpretation. The correct interpretation is that sex is people. Sex-as-biology or sex-as-a-compromise-between-male-and-female-drives is really less than sex. Sex is people, people passionately and physically involved with each other. Thus it is through stories, not abstractions, that we learn what sex really means.

Universal stories
The Bible tells at least two universal stories of marriage. By "universal," I mean stories in which we all can recognize ourselves. They are, in a way, God's stories about sex.

The first is a highly romantic love story. The Bible does not begin to speak about sex with "Thou shalt not," but with this account of joyful, sensual abandon in the Garden of Eden.

It starts, like all stories, with a problem. The first chapter of Genesis reverberates with the regular drumbeat of "good" as God creates the universe. At each stage he looks it over and pronounces his pleasure. But then he announces something unsatisfactory. "It is *not good* that man should be alone" (Gen. 2:18). God's society was inadequate for Adam; he needed the company of another creature. In solving this problem, God presented all the animals to Adam as potential partners. None was found suitable.

So God made a partner for Adam—Eve—and presented her to him. Adam's reaction was immediate and passionate. "This is now bone of my bones and flesh of my flesh" (Gen. 2:23). He felt kinship, and it drew him to her.

Sometimes it is claimed that marriage offers intimate possibilities because of the differences between the sexes—the way in which male and female, as opposites, complement each other. The Genesis story brings a very different emphasis. Of course the two are different: they were even made differently. Yet it was because of their similarity, not because of their differences, that they were drawn to become intimate partners in the garden.

For intimate partners is what they became, summarized in lovely and unforgettable terms: "The man and his wife were both naked, and they felt no shame" (Gen. 2:25).

Genesis 1:27 relates this community of male and female to God himself: "And God created man in his own image, in the image of God he created him; male and female he created them." Something of God is seen in Adam and Eve. As Adam could delight in Eve because she was like him, so God finds particular delight in this man and woman because together they are like him. There is fellowship among the three. This is the fundamental idealism of sexuality that Eden introduces.

It is a brief sketch of a story, yet one we all recognize, because we have lived it—at least in our dreams. From the time that they first become sexually aware, boys daydream about girls; girls dream about boys. They dream about meeting each other in a kind of Eden, naked and unashamed. The real world of sex and marriage can be dreary and heartless, but the hope of replicating Eden begins anew with each generation.

The origins of marriage

Having reported Adam's passionate reaction to Eve—"this is bone of my bones"—Genesis goes on to say, "For this reason a man will leave his father and his mother and be united to his wife, and they will become one flesh" (Gen. 2:24). This verse would later be quoted by both Jesus and Paul. It is not a comment on Adam and Eve, who had no parents, but on marriage as a persistent human institution. Marriage is a remarkable fact of all civilizations—most remarkable of all when seen against a tribal background, in which ties of children to their parents are tremendously strong.

What is stronger than the link between children and their parents? The link between a man and a woman, who forsake their parents for an outsider, with whom they become "one flesh." And why do they undertake this tremendous social revolution? The cause can be found in Adam's spontaneous reaction: *This* is my kind of creature. With her, I can be at home. Humans were made for unashamed nakedness—intimacy seems a weak word to describe it. Longing for it, we marry.

And usually we have children. Genesis does not mention procreation in the verse explaining the fundamental motive for marriage. Rather, childbearing is mentioned in the first chapter of Genesis, as a command in the context of a blessing: "And God blessed them; and God said to them, 'Be fruitful and multiply, and fill the earth, and subdue it' " (1:28).

We do not marry to have children, but to bond to "bone of my bones." God calls married people, however, to the responsibility (and blessing) of children. Does this mean it would be wrong for a couple to decide never to have children? It means at least that a couple ought to have a very good reason for such a choice. Marriage and procreation are meant to go together.

We ought to remember, however, that the command to be fruitful was given when birth control did not exist. The command had nothing to do with the Pill. Rather, for Adam and Eve the command must have meant: Enjoy sex with each other, and be careful to care for, protect, and train the children God gives you as a result. God affirmed that children were part of his blessing, and part of the task given to a man and a woman.

I have heard elderly people, both men and women, say that having and raising children was the most significant thing they did with their lives. Children give us a sense of making progress in the world, of "subduing" the Earth, as God commanded Adam and Eve to do (Gen. 1:28). Husband and wife share this sense of significance, and it draws them closer together. The "one flesh" of sexual intercourse gains a wider and deeper meaning as the two partners work out a shared life—including the shared work of children.

So, in Eden's story, Adam ultimately recognized his wife as more than "bone of my bones." While remaining a joy to him, she would become more—a source of life to others. It was this realization that impelled him to give her the beautiful name "Eve," or "living" (Gen. 3:20).

Eden's story resonates in our experience this way, too. Marriage begins with a small, closed circle: a woman, a man, and the God who gives them to each other. Their eyes are only on each other. "This is bone of my bones." Yet God has a greater blessing in store for them. He lifts their eyes beyond each other. As partners he invites them to "subdue the earth," that is, to create a humane society. As bearers of God's image they are to impress his image on all that surrounds them. Marriage begins with the impulsive longing for another, but comes to the creative task of shaping the world. We do it through children, work, church, neighborhood, through public service. We do it together.

Desire and domination
Unfortunately, Adam and Eve's story did not end in the garden. They sinned, and their estrangement from God marred their partnership. The curse God pronounced to Eve suggests a result with which we are too well familiar: "Your desire will be for your husband, and he will rule over you" (Gen. 3:16). As Derek Kidner has put it, "to love and to cherish" became "to desire and to dominate." So it has been ever since: intimacy trying to find a way to coexist with sex drives and assertions of power.

What exactly changed? Did sin affect the physical nature of their sex life? Augustine imagined that it must have, since he could not imagine God pronouncing good on the kind of sex Augustine knew. He imagined edenic sex as without passion. "With calmness of mind and with no corrupting of the integrity of the body, the husband would lie upon the bosom of his wife. . . . No wild heat of passion would arouse those parts of the body, but a spontaneous power, according to the need, would be present. . . . Thus not the eager desire of lust, but the normal exercise of the will, should join the male and female for breeding and conception." This does not sound, to modern people, like much fun. In fact, it does not sound much like sex. It sounds like a theologian's strained attempt to honor the name of sex without admitting its true character.

Augustine's idea of passionless sex is an easy target. Could he not see that Adam's first reaction to Eve was a far cry from this? Nothing in Scripture suggests that passion came after Eden. There are other explanations of what changed with the Fall. Mary Stewart Van Leeuwen suggests that sin manifests itself in gender roles: the male desire to dominate, the female willingness to accommodate and evade responsibility. Others have speculated that the male tendency to fantasize about depersonalized bodies—shown in the distinctively male penchant for *Playboy* and *Penthouse*—may have originated at the Fall.

What clearly did change was the human being's definition of himself. Ever after Eden he would think of himself as a self-driven god, treating other human beings, his own body, and even God as instruments for his own pleasure. Where once he shared in fellowship with his spouse and his God, now he thinks of himself as over and against them. It is as though they had been made by him and for him alone; their role is to make him happy. That is why, from his point of view, they exist. When they fail to live up to his expectations, he is angry or hurt. After Adam, people hide from God because they fear he will interfere with their happiness; after Adam, they blame their spouse for their failings. The result is too often the "not good" of Eden—for each person is alone again.

The examples are everywhere, if we want to look for them. The man chasing a beautiful woman to gain ego satisfaction and bodily pleasure. The group of women making points for themselves by disparaging their husbands. The boy who has conceived a child but considers it the girl's problem, not his. The wife and husband not speaking to each other, each furious for the other's failure to provide happiness. All of us, in all our interactions, slide toward regarding others as mere instruments for our pleasure. The story of Eden, of mutual unashamed nakedness, of passionate joy in discovering another, of the shared task of children and "subduing the earth," is thoroughly confused by this contrary story of people who think, each one, that they are gods, knowing good and evil without anyone's— least of all God's—direction.

The second story
The Old Testament tells another universal love story: the marriage of God to his people. In this story, like the story of Adam and Eve, all people on Earth can recognize themselves. But this love story, coming after the Fall, bears little resemblance to the passionate happiness of Eden. It is definitely a marriage of passion, but it is equally a marriage that can only be called "hard." It is not a happy

marriage, nor does it seem that there is any earthly hope it will
become one. Perhaps one might as well go all the way to calling it a
bad marriage.

This will, I know, sound harsh and strange to many, who are used
to thinking of God's relationship to his people as a model. It is a
model, but an extremely realistic model. It is a model of how to live
in a hard relationship. The most notable characteristic of this
marriage is the unfaithfulness of the bride, and the passionate,
tortured response of the husband. When the marriage of God to
Israel is described in the Old Testament, it nearly always provokes a
torrent of angry words. Take Jeremiah, for example, as he cites
God's accusations against his beloved. Listen to these words as
though you were overhearing angry taunts through thin apartment
walls:

> " 'I remember the devotion of your youth,
>   how as a bride you loved me
> and followed me through the desert. . . .'
> "Consider then and realize how evil and bitter it is for you
>   when you forsake the Lord your God and have no awe of
>   me,"
>   declares the Lord,
>   the LORD Almighty.
> ". . . Indeed, on every high hill
>   and under every spreading tree
>   you lay down as a prostitute. . . .
> "How can you say, 'I am not defiled. . . '?
> . . . You are a swift she-camel
>   running here and there,
> a wild donkey accustomed to the desert,
>   sniffing the wind in her craving—
>   in her heat who can restrain her?
> Any males that pursue her need not tire themselves;
>   at mating time they will find her. . . .
>
> "[Y]ou have lived as a prostitute with many lovers—
>   would you now return to me?"
>   declares the LORD (Jeremiah 2:2, 19–20, 23–24
>   and 3:1).

Or consider the even rougher language of Ezekiel, Jeremiah's
contemporary:

" 'You adulterous wife! You prefer strangers to your own husband! Every prostitute receives a fee, but you give gifts to all your lovers, bribing them to come to you. . . .
" 'Therefore I am going to gather all your lovers, with whom you found pleasure, those you loved as well as those you hated. I will gather them against you from all around and will strip you in front of them, and they will see your nakedness. I will bring upon you the blood vengeance of my wrath and jealous anger. Then I will hand you over to your lovers. . . . They will strip you of your clothes and take your fine jewelry and leave you naked and bare. They will bring a mob against you, who will stone you and hack you to pieces with their swords' " (Ezekiel 16).

Yet these terrible words—and they are typical of many in the prophets—are interlaced with pleading love:

" *'Return, faithless Israel,' declares the LORD,*
'I will frown on you no longer,
for I am merciful,' declares the LORD
'I will not be angry forever.
Only acknowledge your guilt. . . .'
"Return, faithless people," declares the LORD "for I am your husband' " (Jer. 3:12–14).

The fury of God toward his bride is dreadful. He is not going to live meekly with his wife's infidelity. He cannot. He loves her too much, and he has too much self-respect. He will never be content with a bad marriage; he will rage against it until it is changed.

This ought to do away with any simplistic application of Philippians 2 (about imitating Christ's humility) to marriage. Many wives, particularly, have been told that the godly approach to an unfaithful or abusive partner is quiet patience. Sometimes they can only pray, hope, and endure, it is said.

God is no model of that. Is he quietly patient while his partner abuses his love? He is—about as much as a tornado is a gentle wind. God is not waiting for Israel to see the error of her ways, to be convinced by his Christian love. God demands what he deserves.

A wife who did the same might be accused, by some Christians, of selfishness. And in some cases that would be true. Some marital counseling urges an abused partner to stop worrying about anyone but herself. That, however, is not what God is doing when he demands what he deserves. If God only worried about himself, he would forget Israel utterly. He doesn't "need" Israel. But God loves Israel. Through Israel, furthermore, he wants to redeem the world. Therefore he demands that their marriage become what it was meant to be. To the extent that patience is called for, he is patient. To the extent that his anger may rock Israel from apathy, he is wildly expressive of his anger. Sometimes he initiates a kind of separation, letting Israel experience the result of her own choices. Yet his goal is not in doubt: He will never settle for a bad marriage. He wants a marriage of love and righteousness.

You cannot help seeing, if you consider the whole Bible, that God's humility ultimately dominates. He threatens, blusters, shouts, punishes, he even sends his bride off into exile—but in the end he always goes and brings her back. At any sign of genuine repentance, he throws his arms open to her.

Hope persistently rises in the background—hope that God's love will someday triumph over his wife's indifference. "As a bridegroom rejoices over his bride, so will your God rejoice over you" (Isa. 62:5).

The final word of this love story came in Jesus, who laid aside magisterial power—the power of a husband in patriarchal Israel—and submitted to his wife's rejection. She deserved to die—that was the penalty for adultery—and at the very least she deserved divorce; but he courted her lovingly. He wept for her. These are the words of a lover: "O Jerusalem, Jerusalem, you who kill the prophets and stone those sent to you, how often I have longed to gather your children together, as a hen gathers her chicks under her wings, but you were not willing" (Matt. 23:37). He finally died at her hands. Through this sacrificial act he cleansed her, so that in the end he will gain her again as a radiant bride, unstained by her past (Eph. 5:26–27, Rev. 21:2). The prophets' hopeful vision was fulfilled in Jesus.

Andrew Greeley, who has more sensible things to say than one might expect from reading his steamy romance novels, writes, "The most obvious proof that one does not lose masculinity or strength by exposing one's needs and desires is to be found in Yahweh's making it quite clear how desperately he wants to be loved by his people, and making it clear indeed in explicitly sexual language. If Yahweh can admit that he 'needs' the affection of his beloved, then why should any man be afraid to admit the same thing?" And, Greeley notes, though "making demands" runs against what we have been taught love is, God is clearly a lover unafraid to make demands. "In fact, a love that is not passionate enough to demand the best from the other is not love at all." Love in a bad marriage, if God is a model, is passionate, insistent, aggressive love.

Yet it is also, ultimately, love that will not let go—love that will sacrifice its own life in order to make the marriage into what it was meant to be.

Lessons

What do we learn from these two love stories? I could make almost endless lists of abstract lessons to take from them. Yet stories, I think, are most profitable used in another way—as mirrors for seeing ourselves.

We are meant to see ourselves in Adam and Eve. I can remember thinking, as an adolescent, that if I ever had a woman's body to hold through the night, I would wake each day in a glow of wonder. Such longing is the reason why we marry. Yet how quickly we forget. How quickly we slump into uncommunicative, unappreciative, bad moods. The story of Eden reminds us why we married. It calls us back to our original hope and delight. It is a love story—your love story, mine—to reawaken longing.

We see ourselves in God and Israel, too. Our marriages may be made in Eden, but they do not stay there. They are cast out into the world. They are filled with jealousy, anger, frustration. Why? That is what God wants to know about his marriage. Why would someone take his love for granted? If we could answer the question, we would know why so many of our marriages are lackluster, why so much of our delight in each other becomes covered over with boredom. How is it that two people who once could barely stand to be apart often can barely stand to be together? The only credible answer is the one told in the Genesis story. Wanting to be gods, we have lost our place in Eden.

If you are in a marriage like Israel's, what can give you hope? Is there any possibility that the unashamed nakedness and passionate delight of Eden can be restored? Can this love story have a happy ending? Let us look in the mirror of God and Israel. God perseveres in spite of the pain of rejection. Furthermore, he does not merely "hang in there." He perseveres in hope.

Maybe that hope is irrational. What, after all, would a marriage counselor say to God if he came in for an appointment? From a human point of view, this marriage cannot be saved. But that is precisely why we need the mirror of this story. It tells us that something more than a human point of view is involved in love stories. Somehow, God will make his marriage like the original in Eden, and even better. He wants to save marriages—"save" in the full biblical sense of the word, not merely to preserve from divorce, but to make whole again.

To believe in this possibility takes faith. It is not for the irreligious. That is one reason to tell the story of God and his love for Israel. Stories can excite faith. Stories can inspire. Love stories can get behind our defenses, our busy, small-minded, humdrum pragmatism, and call our hearts toward what we were meant to be. We were meant to be lovers like Adam and Eve—passionate, unashamed. We were meant to be lovers like God—passionate, unwavering even in pain.

When we listen to these stories, we approach marriage in a very different way from the pragmatic secularism of our age. We stop calculating how we can make ourselves happy. We begin seeking to reflect God.

Love that will not let go

Ruth, with whom I began this chapter, has been married for almost ten years, and I have known her well through most of those. They have not been easy years, as I have mentioned. She and her husband are both intense, dedicated, complicated. What causes their troubles? Sex, for one. They often can't get their signals straight, and feelings are hurt over imaginary (or maybe real) rejections. They compete with each other. They hold grudges. But maybe more than any other single problem is this slippery one: Neither one of them knows how to encourage the other. They try, but their attempts are always prickly. When one makes an effort, the other often rebuffs it. You could spend a long time analyzing why, and maybe you would figure it out. But how they are supposed to change is a different matter.

In the last few years I have thought it might be getting better. They have gone to counseling, and they have found some other couples with whom to share a genuine and deep fellowship. Sometimes their marriage really does seem to be better. At other times, it slips back into grudges and embittered silences.

If the purpose of marriage were purely to provide happy intimacy, their marriage might be called purposeless. Oh, sure, it is quite possible they would be as troubled, or even more so, with other partners, or alone. But I suspect they would take their chances. They have stayed married largely because they were brought up to believe that marriage is for life, and that divorce is wrong. Also, I suppose, they are stubborn people. They don't give up easily.

And one more factor: They really do love each other, in their own tormented way. Their own personal legacy of Eden is not entirely used up. They just have not figured out how to turn it into happiness.

It is quite clear to me, however, that happiness is not the chief point of marriage. However happy marriages may be—and many are happy—marriage is a temporary fact of existence on Earth, and cannot be best understood as an end in itself. It is not a mere convenient compromise either. Marriages are important to God, not simply for the happiness they can bring, but because they point beyond themselves.

Marriage is not God's kingdom, but it teaches us what his kingdom is like. As his kingdom is about love, it is natural that marriage should teach us about love. It does this in two ways.

The first way I see quite often in my own marriage. "Easy" marriages shine with the beauty of intimate love, the kind of natural, heartfelt, spontaneous responsiveness that was felt in Eden, that the Song of Songs witnesses to, and that is seen in Jesus' love for the Father. Someday we will attain such a love, I assume, in all our doings. It must be the way everything is done and felt in heaven. For many of us, marriages—our own or others'—are the closest we ever come to understanding such love. Even though we experience love imperfectly, through our love we understand something about the love of God.

But the other way of love is perhaps more normal in this broken world, and I see it in Ruth's marriage. It is love that will not let go, love that will not accept defeat, the love of passionate demands and passionate tears.

Saint John of the Cross wrote that love consists "not in feeling great things, but in suffering for the beloved." Paul told husbands to love their wives as Christ loved the church, and Christ's love found its greatest expression on the cross. For many of us, hard marriages—our own or others'—are the closest we ever come to understanding God's stubborn, passionate love.

Marriages like Ruth's are not happiness, nor are they peace. But they are certainly a sign. Their persistence points beyond themselves, to God. We are loved that way by our Lord. He may not be happy with the marriage. But he is not about to quit.

The possibility of divorce

Is there, then, no possibility of divorce? "In the beginning it was not so," Jesus told the Pharisees (Matt. 19:8). Indeed, it is impossible to imagine divorce in Eden. God joins the two in delight—what could separate them? At best, divorce is an accommodation to the "hardness of heart" that has invaded Eden and forced us out of Eden.

It was not meant to be so, but it is so. Partners abuse each other. Hearts are hardened. Marriages are destroyed. People lose hope. These are realities of human life. Christians differ in their thinking about how to respond to these facts. Some reject any compromise with defeat. They will never accept divorce. Others will choose to accommodate the realities of failed marriages, out of pity for the people involved. There is enough uncertainty in the biblical data for them to justify doing so.

That is not at all the same, however, as viewing divorce as normal. Our society now treats divorce as an ordinary happenstance, like a car breaking down. It is too bad, but these things happen. You try your best, but sometimes it doesn't work out. But for Christians, divorce should be a failure and an aberration from Eden in each and every case. It is always a cause for mourning, not merely because of the personal distress the broken marriage has caused, but because divorce communicates something to the world. It says the partners in the marriage have lost hope, lost faith, lost love, and have quit at something God ordained. People will quit, in a fallen world, and in some way or another we will have to recognize that. But let us not call it anything other than what it is: a failure. It is a failure to make the sign of God's kingdom.

That was precisely the argument Moses made when God, angry at his people, threatened to destroy them and start over. "Then the Egyptians will hear about it! . . . And they will tell the inhabitants of this land about it. . . . If you put these people to death at one time, the nations who have heard this report about you will say, 'The LORD was not able to bring these people into the land he promised them . . .' " (Num. 14:16).

God had every justification to divorce his people. He could not do so, however, without damaging his reputation. Once he had started the marriage, his honor and his love demanded that he finish it. So it is with human marriages. They are not just made up of human choices. God joins the two together. His honor and his love as well as ours is at stake. "What God has joined together, let man not separate." When we do separate them, we give up on God's purposes for them. We make an anti-sign of God's kingdom. It is a sign of Humpty Dumpty, of unredeemable brokenness.

Institutions or individuals?

A man comes to see a marriage counselor. He has been married for twelve years, and he says that all have been unhappy. During the entire twelve years the two have never successfully had intercourse. His wife has vaginismus, a condition that makes intercourse very painful. They have been to counseling together, but it has not helped. He and his wife are committed Christians; the wife does not want a divorce. The husband, however, is ready to quit. He knows that marriage is important, but he says, "I don't believe that God would destroy two individuals in order to preserve an institution."

Put that way, who could disagree? God loves people, not institutions. To anyone who feels for this man and his wife, divorce will seem to be an act of liberating kindness. The twelve-year stalemate will be broken. Finally they will have some relief from the misery! Two individuals will be rescued from an institution that has become a prison. The marriage is a failure; divorce will seem to be a limited triumph—like a successful retreat from a lost battle.

When one thinks more carefully, however, questions arise. These marriage partners will leave one prison—but will they enter another? Their marriage has been miserable because they both suffer from miserable personal problems. Will the net sum of misery decrease because they have gone their own ways? Or will it be compounded by isolation and loneliness as they are separate? Initially, divorce may feel like an improvement, but will it remain so?

Another question: Why have they not had intercourse in twelve years? Vaginismus is treatable. They have been to marriage counseling, but have they really explored all possibilities for healing? Or have they merely made a gesture at getting help, so that forever after they could say, "We tried"?

These quibbles are practical ones. Extended from these two individuals to our whole society, this practical line of thinking would ask, "Have increased divorces made Americans happier?" No one can answer this question precisely, because happiness cannot be measured. However, there is reason to think that a divorce-happy America is not really happier.

But suppose that all practical questions are answered. The man's question remains. Would God destroy two individuals in order to preserve an institution? Of course not. But what do we mean by *destroy?*

A Christian would have to conclude that destroying a person involves more than disturbing his health or his peace of mind. You want to destroy a person? Cut him off from the possibility of meaning. Let him do exactly as he wants—lie by the pool all day reading *People*, or play the stock market for millions—but let his life mean nothing to himself, or to his family or friends.

There have been, obviously, many who suffered (as martyrs, in the extreme case) believing that while suffering they were living at the peak of their existence. Is it possible to suffer in the same way for marriage? Is it possible that the Ephesians 5:25 command, "Husbands, love your wives, just as Christ loved the church and gave himself up for her," applies precisely here?

Thinking of this man in terms of our two primary stories is revealing. He was created to live Adam's story, passionately responding to his wife in joy. But perhaps hardness of heart has destroyed that possibility. If so, what can he do? He can divorce, making the Humpty Dumpty sign. It would be hard to blame him; none of us would want to be in his place. But there is another possibility. He can carry on God's story, refusing to accept a bad marriage, but refusing to give up on it either. He can continue in anger and yet self-sacrifice. Why should he? Because it will make him happy? Because it will preserve an important institution? No, because it will allow him the privilege of making the sign of God's kingdom. He will demonstrate God's passionate persistence. He will show his faith in the possibilities of God redeeming that which he has joined together.

God's story, we must remember, is not ultimately sad. It is not a matter of hanging on without hope. It is a story in which love triumphs in the end. However, in order for the story to end that way, someone had to die undeservingly. We, as Christ's disciples, have been called to share in his sufferings. Surely we cannot exempt marriage from that call. Surely in marriage, as in all of life, Jesus' words ring true: "Whoever loses his life for my sake will find it" (Matt. 10:39).

Chapter 5

JESUS, PAUL, AND BEYOND

*F*or George, faithfulness was a woman's virtue. Before his marriage he sowed plenty of wild oats with a variety of girls of dubious reputations. Then he met Gail. She was the kind of "good girl" a man hoped to marry. On their first date, George did something he had never done with a girl before. He brought her home to meet his mother.

Throughout his married life George continued having affairs. He genuinely loved Gail, but he couldn't imagine restraining his sexual impulses when the opportunity came. By the time they celebrated their twenty-fifth wedding anniversary he had no idea how many different partners he'd enjoyed; there must have been hundreds. He knew, vaguely, that it was wrong, and he always felt penitent when he came home to his wife afterwards. Still, he continued.

On his fifty-sixth birthday, Gail threw him out of the house. She had learned a thing or two from the feminist movement, and had decided she didn't need to put up with his philandering. Her therapist had encouraged her to set some limits, and to stick to them.

For the past four months George has been living in a small, unfurnished apartment. He is terribly lonely. George calls Gail almost every day, and he promises to do better, but she is enjoying her freedom and *says she would like time before they re-establish their relationship. Also, she would like to see how well he can live up to his promises of reform. George makes all kinds of promises, but when he is most truthful, he is not sure how well he can keep them.*

Jesus was born into a world where marriage would never have been confused with Eden. It was a culture in which men routinely abused or cheated on their wives, a society that, though dominated by strict Jewish monogamy, took spin from dissolute Greco-Roman morals. George's behavior would have seemed routine.

What did Jesus have to say to this world about sex? The answer seems to be: not very much. At least, very little of his recorded teaching concerns sex or sexuality.

This was not because he only associated with people of good morals. Rather, Jesus was often found with people on the margins of acceptable society—tax collectors, "sinners," and prostitutes. Jesus' message to them was positive: he proclaimed salvation. He told the religious leaders, in fact, that prostitutes would enter the kingdom of God before they did (Matt. 21:31). He was not speaking hyperbolically. It happened just as Jesus had predicted. Years later Paul could write to the Corinthians, listing various kinds of sexually immoral persons—fornicators, adulterers, male prostitutes, and homosexual offenders—and simply say, "And such were some of you" (1 Cor. 6:11).

It is within this context that we must think about how to minister to George. We may be tempted to deal only with his marital and sexual problems. But these problems have been invaded by a saving reality: Jesus has come into the world. George does not merely need to straighten up. He needs to experience Jesus' salvation.

Jesus and the Old Testament
When he did talk about sex, Jesus usually stayed within the Old Testament tradition. He was not, by and large, an innovator in sexual ethics. He underscored the Old Testament teaching that marriage was the only place for sex. If anything, he was stricter. He closed the divorce loophole: For a man to marry and divorce a series of wives was not, he taught, acceptable, however legal it might be. (The Mosaic law permitted divorce, but Jesus' view of marriage drew more from such Old Testament passages as Malachi 2:16: " 'I

hate divorce,' says the LORD God of Israel.") Jesus was not satisfied with superficial marital faithfulness. He demanded faithfulness of the heart. A man who lusted after other women, he said, was equivalent to an adulterer (Matt. 5:27-28).

Some have understood Jesus to mean, in his comment on lust, that all sexual desire or fantasy is illegitimate. That would have been a new teaching, without Old Testament parallel. But the interpretation stretches the evidence. "Lust" is a broad word in New Testament Greek, whose meaning depends on the context. It can more accurately be translated "strongly desire." It is sometimes used in a positive context. (For instance, Jesus' words in Luke 22:15 can be translated, literally, "I have *lusted* to eat this Passover with you." Evidently such lust was not wrong, nor is it likely Jesus was referring to his own mental fantasies about the meal.)

Jesus' comment on mental adultery refers not to fantasies but to desire. He might be paraphrased this way: "To want what is wrong sexually is just as evil as to do what is wrong sexually." He was concerned, here as elsewhere, with purity of heart. There is nothing wrong with a person who admires and is sexually attracted to other persons. There is much wrong with a person who has, perhaps over a period of time, oriented his mind toward a person who has not been given to him. Attraction is a healthy sensual and aesthetic reaction; sinful lust is an enduring drive that captures the mind.

Jesus' words are closely linked to the tenth commandment, "You shall not covet . . . your neighbor's wife" (Exod. 20:17). Since "your neighbor's wife" is included in a list of the neighbor's property, the tenth commandment is sometimes thought to be a protection of property rights. Not so. Coveting your neighbor's property does no harm to your neighbor. It does harm to you, by inflaming your desire for something that has not been given to you.

In the kingdom of God, a person will want what God gives. His mind and his body will be oriented toward that single love. A person whose mind dwells longingly on a sexual temptation is not merely in danger of going wrong; he has already gone wrong. He wants what is not his to have. He may be outwardly faithful, but his heart is unfaithful.

There can be few whom this teaching does not condemn. We *do* want what is not ours. If we were not prisoners of sin, we would not have needed Jesus' help. Jesus' uniqueness was not (or at least not only) in his ethical teaching, but in his offering of salvation from sin.

What Jesus told his audiences of sinners, tax collectors, and prostitutes—as well as Pharisees, centurions, rich young men, beggars, leprosy victims, and all the rest—was "the kingdom of God is near" (Mark 1:15). He showed very little interest in reforming the sexual morals of society. He poured all his efforts into communicating the way in which God was about to turn society upside-down. He called people to enter his new society, and live in a new way.

Jesus as celibate

In one way, especially, Jesus was an innovator standing utterly apart from the Old Testament. He was celibate. There have been speculations that he might have married earlier in his life, but they fail to explain credibly why no wife or children are mentioned in the Gospels. His disciples, furthermore, were called to leave their wives and families when they followed him.

He lived a celibacy without asceticism. He talked freely with women from all walks of life. He drank wine and was criticized for it. He celebrated a wedding, and honored it with a gift of wine. (What a curiosity, that his first miracle should be "wasted" on such a frivolous gesture!) Though he lived by charity, he ate what was put before him. He did not teach a dietary regimen, such as vegetarianism. He was anything but a hermit, and his disciples were activists in the world they inhabited. There is no trace of antimaterial feeling in the Gospels, not even in the account of the Virgin Birth, which is recounted as a miraculous sign, not as a preference for God's Son to be conceived without sex. (The line from "O Come All Ye Faithful"— "Lo, he abhors not the Virgin's womb"—would never have occurred to first-century Christians.) Contrast this with the Buddha's virgin birth: His mother was said to have died seven days after his birth because "it is not fitting that she who bears a Peerless One should afterwards indulge in love." Such thinking invaded the Christian church generations afterwards, and Mary's perpetual virginity ultimately became dogma; but there is no hint of that kind of anti-sexuality in the gospel.

Yet Jesus was celibate. For him, the "traditional family" was not equivalent to the kingdom of God. He taught that there is no marriage in heaven. As we have noted, he taught that the gospel must sometimes divide and alienate families.

Jesus believed in the idealism of Eden, nonetheless. He quoted from Genesis, and added the comment: "What God has joined together, let no man separate" (Matt. 19:6). Marriage was not a man-made institution, for him; each and every marriage was a bond joined by God.

Yet, in the very same passage, Jesus commented that not everyone was meant for marriage. Some might be "eunuchs" because of their birth or experience, and some might make themselves "eunuchs" for the sake of the kingdom of heaven (19:12). A radical new element was introduced by Jesus, something beyond Eden and its ideal of male and female cleaving together, naked and unashamed.

Jesus said little to explain celibacy. He did not remark on why God's comment in Genesis 2:18, "It is not good for man to be alone," did not apply. He simply lived a style of life that was completely committed to ministry, and unencumbered by family (or house, or job). He called his disciples to the same style of life during the time they were with him.

The New Testament Epistles

Paul, perhaps even more than Jesus, ministered to people with sexual problems, for many of his converts were Gentiles. The Greco-Roman culture offered few boundaries for men, who cultivated a variety of sexual relationships with their wives, with slaves of both sexes, with concubines, with boys, and with prostitutes both secular and sacred. A particular kind of sexual relationship—homosexual or heterosexual, married or unmarried—was not right or wrong; what was right or wrong was a man's sexual style. He was to demonstrate moderation and self-mastery, whatever the sexual practice.

We know more about Paul's thinking on sex than we know about Jesus', for Paul wrote letters to churches struggling with sexual issues. Like Jesus, Paul affirmed the Old Testament tradition, yet expanded on it. For example, he affirmed that God was against incest (1 Cor. 5:1), and that believers ought never to marry outside the community of faith (1 Cor. 7:39, 2 Cor. 6:14). He was against homosexuality (Romans 1).

Perhaps Paul's most remarkable teaching on sexuality came in Ephesians 5:22–33. Some people say that Paul was antimarriage. They cannot have thought much about the implications of this passage. For Paul, the most astonishing fact in the universe was

God's love for his people, exemplified in Christ. Marriage was parallel to that, Paul said. Marriage was meant to reflect the relationship of Christ and the church.

A thought exercise: Suppose you are the apostle Paul. Your task is to write about marriage in the most extravagantly exalted way possible. Can you think of a parallel that would give marriage any higher status than this one implies?

Paul's idealism would have been very strange to Greeks, who regarded the wife as very strictly the servant and property of her husband. For Jews, the comparison must have been easier to appropriate. The prophets Hosea, Jeremiah, and Ezekiel had developed, centuries before, the parallel between marriage and God's love for Israel.

The prophets, however, had used the comparison in a way that did not necessarily raise the status of marriage. They said God's relationship to Israel was like a marriage to an unfaithful woman.

Paul applied the same parallel in the opposite direction. Rather than describing heaven in terms of what we know on Earth, he said that Earth should reflect what we know of heaven. Marriages ought to reflect God's love for his people, Paul urged. Men's love for their wives ought to echo the character and action of God. Women ought to respond to their husbands in the same way they knew it right to respond to Christ. Not only was the application reversed, but Paul painted a much brighter picture than had the prophets. For Paul, Christ's love for his church was triumphant. Whatever frustration God had experienced was now history. His love would transform his bride into a woman "without stain or wrinkle or any other blemish, but holy and blameless" (Eph. 5:27).

One flesh

A second development from the Old Testament was Paul's explanation of "one flesh." In Genesis 2:24, "one flesh" was an aspect of marriage: "For this reason a man will leave his father and mother and be united to his wife, and they will become one flesh." Jesus interpreted this as more than a purely human phenomenon. He saw God joining together the man and woman. "What God has joined together, let man not separate" (Matt. 19:6). But when Paul wrote to the Corinthian church, he had in mind a very different sort of situation: impersonal, commercialized sex.

Even in that situation, in which no love or commitment was involved, in which names were unnecessary, Paul emphatically claimed that sexual intercourse bonded the two people. But this was not a God-made unity that should never be broken; it was an antispiritual unity that ought to be escaped as quickly as possible. God did not join these people; sex did.

Paul is sometimes accused of setting the human body against our spiritual nature, and teaching that one must rise above the body into the spiritual realm. But here, Paul makes clear that no one rises above the body. The Corinthians would have liked to think of bodily actions—including sex—as spiritually irrelevant. Paul insists that sex has implications no one can escape. "All other sins a man commits are outside his body, but he who sins sexually sins against his own body" (1 Cor. 6:18).

Paul is using the word *body* the way we might use the word *person*. His point is that sexual sin is never a "victimless crime." The people involved are victims. When they unite themselves unsuitably, they pollute themselves. Lewis Smedes says it eloquently: "It does not matter what the two people have in mind. The whore sells her body with an unwritten understanding that nothing personal will be involved in the deal. . . . The buyer gets his sexual needs satisfied without having anything personally difficult to deal with after-wards. . . . But none of this affects Paul's point. The *reality* of the act, unfelt and unnoticed by them, is this: it unites them—body and soul—to each other. . . ." You cannot act as though sex has no great meaning at all. Sex always has deep personal implications. You cannot, Paul says, treat it as mere recreation.

Though Paul applied this in a negative context, he was giving sex itself a powerful, positive meaning. For Paul, sex was not merely a source of pleasure, nor merely a way to express love. Intercourse was an act with its own built-in meaning. It unified the two who were sexually involved, for good or, as in the Corinthians' case, for evil. To evaluate a particular act of sexual intercourse, one would need to know who were involved, and what they planned to do with the unity sex brings. But there was no such thing as meaningless sex.

Paul on celibacy

A third concern for Paul was celibacy. Writing to the Corinthians, he recommended marriage as a necessity for some, but thought celibacy better for those who were capable of controlling themselves. (Paul labors to qualify this recommendation as his view, not one he has from the Lord.) There was no Old Testament preparation for this. For Old Testament Israel, marriage was obligatory for everyone.

In 1 Corinthians 7, Paul takes a very practical view of sexuality within marriage. For both men and women, intercourse is a duty owed to a spouse, to protect him or her from temptation. (Notably, it is a mutual, equal duty—the woman's sexual rights are the same as the man's.) Paul's view here is distinctively pragmatic, compared to the comments he makes in the previous chapter. Marriage is necessary for some people, he says, to keep them out of trouble.

Some commentators have concluded from this that he held a very low view of marriage. Historian Lawrence Stone notes in passing, "As is well known, St. Paul put marriage far below virginity in terms of morality, a mere reluctant compromise to deal with the problem of concupiscence." If Paul wrote Ephesians, though, this "well known" is unjustifiable. Clearly, Paul had a remarkably high view of marriage. In any case, 1 Corinthians 7 is not a low view of marriage, but a practical view. For some people, Paul recognized, sexual desires are best met within marriage.

First Corinthians 7 does not offer a low view of marriage, but a high view of celibacy. Some have attributed this to Greek asceticism, alien to Jewish thought. But Paul's reasoning is very different from the ascetic's. He is not recommending celibacy in order to beat down "the flesh." Elsewhere he has harsh words for those who "forbid people to marry and order them to abstain from certain foods. . . . For everything God created is good, and nothing is to be rejected if it is received with thanksgiving . . ." (1 Tim. 4:3–4). Those are not the words of an ascetic, nor really are those found in 1 Corinthians 7:

> Because of the present crisis, I think that it is good for you to remain as you are. Are you married? Do not seek a divorce. Are you unmarried? Do not look for a wife. But if you do marry, you have not sinned; and if a virgin marries, she has not sinned. But those who marry will face many troubles in this life, and I want to spare you this.
>
> What I mean, brothers, is that the time is short. From now on those who have wives should live as if they had none; those who mourn, as if they did not; those who are happy, as

if they were not; those who buy something, as if it were not theirs to keep; those who use the things of the world, as if not engrossed in them. For this world in its present form is passing away.

I would like you to be free from concern. An unmarried man is concerned about the Lord's affairs—how he can please the Lord. But a married man is concerned about the affairs of this world—how he can please his wife—and his interests are divided. An unmarried woman or virgin is concerned about the Lord's affairs: Her aim is to be devoted to the Lord in both body and spirit. But a married woman is concerned about the affairs of this world—how she can please her husband. I am saying this for your own good, not to restrict you, but that you may live in a right way in undivided devotion to the Lord (vv. 26–35).

The thing to note particularly is Paul's middle paragraph. He says that in light of the soon-to-come judgment, everything on Earth should be viewed as temporary and conditional. Living in such a transitional period, a Christian must choose a style of service. He can concentrate on serving God within the temporal—in marriage, particularly—or he can turn his attention more directly to the coming kingdom and the "glorious freedom of the children of God" (Rom. 8:21). Paul says both choices are good, but in his judgment the latter is better.

If the Corinthians were being persecuted, that might partly explain why Paul prefers celibacy. Certainly the difficulties of family life would be increased under such circumstances. But Paul's judgment is not mainly concerned with the difficulties of married life; rather, he is concerned with the freedom possible for the man or woman living in "undivided devotion to the Lord." Paul favors the kind of positive commitment that he himself had made. All his energy went toward advancing God's kingdom. He would go anywhere and suffer anything for this. Paul perceived his style of life as a joy. Preaching and prayer were an incomparable feast. Anything else, even the joys of married life, would compete with that chiefest joy.

One must stretch considerably to blame Greek asceticism for Paul's teaching about celibacy. His authority was nearer to hand: Jesus taught about celibacy, and lived a celibate life. In Bethlehem,

something new was born. Both the old Jewish order and the sur-
rounding Greco-Roman culture were radicalized by the invasion of
the kingdom of God. Paul favored celibacy because he believed it
joyfully in tune with the opportunities of that new reality.

*Judith grew up in a Baptist church, attending the requisite years of
Sunday school. She can't remember any lesson that dealt specifically
with sex, yet somehow she received a very clear idea of what God had to
say on the subject. "What it amounted to was, 'Don't.' Don't do
anything. Whatever it is you'd like to do, it's probably wrong."*

*When she was entering high school, she became more curious about
what the Bible actually said about sex. "I remember taking down my
father's big black Bible, which had all these notes and indexes and
charts. I expected, I guess, that sex would be warned against on about
every other page. But I searched that Bible from beginning to end, as
best I could, and I was really puzzled that I couldn't find much on the
subject at all. All I found were a few verses that were fairly vague—I
mean, they didn't actually say whether petting was wrong. They said
things like, 'Flee fornication,' and I wasn't actually very clear on what
fornication meant. I thought I must be missing something, but I was
too embarrassed to ask anybody for help. It wasn't until many years
later, after I was married and had children, that the idea occurred to me
that maybe God wasn't as preoccupied with sex as I had thought."*

When someone like Judith looks for answers about sex in the Bible,
she usually has to scour the Bible, and sometimes twist it, to find
answers. The Bible shows limited interest in our sexual agenda.

Imagine Jesus presenting his Sermon on the Mount in the way we
would have liked him to:

"Blessed are husbands who are sensitive to the needs of their
wives, for they shall reap sexual satisfaction one hundredfold.

"Blessed are wives who develop an inner sense of worth, for they
shall pass on self-worth to their children, who are the future of
Israel.

"Blessed are teenagers who wait for marriage, for they shall build
strong families after they get their education."

Or imagine Paul, beginning his talk on Mars Hill by saying, "Men
of Athens, I see that in every way you are concerned about the
stability of society. Yet homosexuality, prostitution, and casual sex

run rampant. I want to talk to you about how the Lord Jesus Christ can help you build strong marriages, and help your children grow up with self-esteem."

Manifestly, that was not what Jesus or Paul proclaimed to the world. They preached the kingdom of God. When they spoke or wrote about issues of sexuality, it was nearly always within the context of the question, "What should the life of a community belonging to God look like?" They were, in this way, too, consistent with the Old Testament. The laws given at Sinai were for God's chosen people. No prophet would have thought of proclaiming them to Babylon or Egypt. If foreigners were to hear any message, it would have to be: "Submit to the God of Israel."

The new community
The radical influence of the early Christians began with the conversion of individuals to Christ. Converts were enfolded into the family of the church. And in this church, certain standards of behavior were expected, as a way of living up to the new thing that had happened.

This new community of believers changed the world, including its sexuality. Historians are at a loss to understand why Christianity swept through the Mediterranean. They are equally at a loss to understand how it transformed Greco-Roman sexual mores. Unquestionably, it did. Lawrence Stone summarizes: "Whatever the cause of this great moral mutation, which at the moment remains obscure, the result was a shift from a bisexual world divided between the penetrators and the penetrated, to one divided between reproductive heterosexuality and sterile homosexuality; from one of marriage as a relatively rare legal condition undertaken for purposes of property disposal and inheritance, to marriage as a normal condition of that great majority of mankind unable to live a life of total chastity; from one of ethically neutral male bisexual promiscuity in marriage, to an ideal of male and female marital fidelity; from the moral acceptability of the use of slaves against their own wills as sexual playthings, to a new universal code of sexual behavior no longer dependent upon the status of the parties involved; and finally from incest as merely a sin to incest as against nature."

I have found it encouraging, as a Christian in the twentieth century, to read about these and other changes. For the mores of the ancient Greeks remind me more than a little of my own time. At some points, that ancient Greek culture sounds like what the sexual revolution is aiming for. The Greeks were completely absorbed by questions of the right style of sexual involvement, the proper cultivation of pleasure, the meticulous care of the self. Their flexible concerns seem more attractive than severe Christian morals. Yet Greek ethics collapsed in the face of the Christian challenge.

A revolution of hope

But my point is not that Christianity reshaped society's sexual mores. It did, but for Christians these changes were merely eddies from a much larger wave of change: their personal recognition of Christ as Lord. For the Jew it meant abandoning hope in a temporal government with headquarters in Jerusalem, and recognizing tiny, persecuted churches flung out across the world as the seed from which the New Jerusalem would grow. For the Gentile it meant abandoning mystical philosophies, and centering his hope on a single man known to have been executed by the Roman authorities in Palestine.

One would never have mistaken Christianity for a way to shore up society. It challenged the foundations of society: worship of the emperor and respect for philosophy, in the Greco-Roman world, devotion to the temple and to the Law in the Jewish world.

Christianity did not offer safety in a changing world, but hope. It was a revolution of hope. The kingdom of God has broken in, it announced. The churches were its outposts. One might not see much glory in these tiny, scattered churches; not many Christians, said the apostle Paul, were wise, influential, or from the upper class (1 Cor. 1:26). But they celebrated the triumph of eternal life over death. They announced the victory of love, not in some ethereal sense, but in a tangible, historical sense.

Fairly often this was explained in political language, in terms of "lordship" and the kingdom of God. Yet it was also explained in sexual language. Paul referred to the church as the bride of Christ, promised as a virgin to her husband. Jesus told parables about the kingdom of God being like a wedding to which guests are invited (Matt. 22:1–14; Luke 14:8–11). Another parable compared the kingdom to ten virgins waiting at night for the arrival of the bridegroom for a wedding banquet (Matt. 25:1). At another time, Jesus referred to himself as a bridegroom; all must celebrate so long as he is present (Luke 5:34).

These metaphors speak vividly of God's passion for his people. The love is not yet fully realized—the marriage is not consummated—but the plan is announced, the bride readies herself, the two await the fullness of their love. Revelation depicts the new heaven and new earth this way: "I saw the Holy City, the new Jerusalem, coming down out of heaven from God, prepared as a bride beautifully dressed for her husband" (Rev. 21:2).

Salvation is, finally, the marriage of God to humanity. This is the radical announcement that changed the world: The obstructions are removed; the match is made.

The difference salvation makes
In the new Jerusalem, our sexuality will be transformed. There is no human marriage there; our sexuality will be, presumably, quite different from what we experience now. Will we still *be* sexual? Possibly that question can best be answered with another: How could we not be? We were made, male and female, in God's image, and that image can only be intensified in heaven, not erased. I do not know what to anticipate, but I believe that maleness will be more male, and femaleness more female, and that the community we enjoy will be richer and deeper. What we will look like, or what we will do, I have no idea. But we will be sexual, since we were made sexual.

In the meantime, salvation has already broken into our lives. What are the implications, sexually? How should this affect George and Gail, with whom I began this chapter? I would put it quite simply: The love of God works to make us able to love and be loved. The choices of the Fall—of self-assertion and independence—are being reversed. God is making us into people who choose to love and be loved by him, giving all of ourselves to him in passionate surrender.

Many people have noticed how close the language of mysticism and eroticism often become. (Saint Teresa wrote very graphically of being "ravished" by Christ.) And why not? Both are languages of passionate love. The love of God is not the same as the love of human beings. But if we are made in his image, they cannot be utterly dissimilar, either.

If we learn to love and be loved by God, we become better able to love and be loved by other people. We ought to become better married partners. We ought to become better friends and coworkers.

The fruit of the Spirit, which flow from the joyful marriage of God and humanity, are the very qualities every human relationship must have to live: love, joy, peace, patience, kindness, goodness, faithfulness, gentleness and self-control.

Loving relationships require risk. To love is to expose yourself and risk humiliation. God's love makes it possible. We know that no one who is in Christ will ever be put to shame. Within the security Jesus offers, we can be brave enough to risk being "naked and not ashamed" before each other.

Loving relationships require forgiveness. If we have experienced forgiveness from God, we ought to be able to forgive and be forgiven by a spouse, a friend, or a coworker.

Loving relationships require faithfulness. The faithfulness and single-mindedness in which God trains his disciples—the fidelity to our vows to him—is the same quality that marriage demands. Friendship too, though its commitments are more limited, requires such fidelity and trustworthiness.

Loving relationships require hope, which God inspires. The certainty of a future in Christ, which enables us to endure hardships of all kinds in following him, ought to fill us with hope when we consider our human relationships. How can we stick to them, filled as they may be with bitterness, frustration and disappointment? We can do it only in the certainty that we are all being changed—that if we endure, we will see bitterness drawn like poison from a wound.

George and Gail

But George and Gail *are* Christians. At least, they have in recent years made a commitment to Christ. They are faithful church members. Yet salvation has not transformed their relationship.

Why not? One reason is that George and Gail have only recently begun to experience Christ's influence. They are new Christians, and they are just beginning to understand how Jesus wants to change their sexual and marital lives. It never before occurred to George to attempt marital faithfulness. Now he is trying. It takes time to undo fifty years of training in unfaithfulness.

What about Christians who committed their lives long ago? They may have severe problems, too. Perhaps theirs are not the same problems that George and Gail have, but they are problems nonetheless. Why are they not transformed?

Perhaps it is because they go it alone. Counseling may be available before they marry, and when they are deeply in trouble; but on a daily basis, the church almost entirely leaves out their sexuality. Its counsel is limited to a handful of "Don'ts." Sex just isn't talked about. Compare this with the situation in Corinth, where Paul obviously was quite familiar with the sexual problems of church members and could address them publicly.

We are daily influenced by our culture. In order to be transformed by Christ, we need a counterculture. We need to become a community that channels Christ's salvation into practical terms. This is not simply for our practical good. We do not want to go back to confusing family life with the kingdom of God. Rather, we want our lives transformed by Christ in order that they may reflect his greater glory.

Every created thing is made to give praise to God—the birds, the rocks, the fields. All of them refer us to their Maker and his goodness. So should our sexuality. That seemed to be Paul's particular interest when he wrote to the Corinthians. He was not concerned with sexual ethics for their own sake. He was concerned about the Corinthians as people devoted to Christ. How should their sexual behavior affect them as a worshiping and witnessing community? How should their sexual behavior affect them in their devotion to Christ? How should their sexual behavior affect those to whom they witness? That is the starting point for Christian sexual ethics: how does the people of God live in a way that is worthy of God?

Chapter 6

THE BOUNDARIES AROUND LOVE

*J*ames's life is a mess. He is on his third marriage, and it has about as much hope as a possum frozen in the lights of a semitruck. Three weeks ago Judy moved to another state with a woman she met at a weekend seminar on inner illumination. James languishes in bars after work, hoping to pick up a girl; but he always ends up playing video games and drinking too much. "My life is just a country-western song," he says, and thinks that's some kind of original line.

He doesn't really care who knows. He'll talk about it to anybody. One time, though, he was pouring out his story to someone he'd met on the train going into the city. The guy had really seemed interesting until he began talking about his church and inviting James to attend.

"That's one place I'll never go, no matter how far down I get," James swears fervently. "Religion is just a big guilt trip. I don't need their guilt. I don't need their rules."

Sometimes it appears only one serious sin is left in America: narrow-mindedness. Every other wrongdoing can be understood, accepted, psychologized, therapized. But there is no excuse for considering other people sinners.

This puts Christians in a difficult position. We cannot hide the unmistakable scriptural prominence of rules. Nor can we avoid applying rules. We must call other people, as well as ourselves, to acknowledge their sinfulness.

Certainly, rules are not the heart of our message, though Christians sometimes give that unfortunate impression. Our message is not the law, which only condemns, but the good news of salvation. Still, the good news without the law's requirements becomes merely cheap grace. Certainly, too, sin goes deeper than rules. Sin is a condition of the whole person. Someone may be outwardly flawless yet inwardly rotten. This was Jesus' chief criticism of the Pharisees: they had failed to understand how deep and intractable sin was. By defining it superficially, they had managed to make themselves look good.

Yet Jesus did not do away with rules. He condemned anyone who would remove the slightest of the law's demands. The rules cannot give life. They never saved anyone. In the sexual realm, obeying the rules will not guarantee a faithful marriage or a fruitful single life. Yet rules are part of the Christian witness about sexuality. The law—which certainly includes rules—is a teacher and a guide toward salvation. We cannot be saved without it.

Setting some standards

For people like James the question is not whether a particular rule can be justified; the question is whether any rule can be justified. They would like to live free of all constraints. They won't tolerate anybody "judging" them.

Yet every important area of life is ruled by some standards. James, for instance, would never pay money for sex; he considers prostitution demeaning. It is true that he would not apply his standard to anyone else; whatever others enjoy is their business, he says. (He would probably except incest or child abuse, since they involve coercion.) Yet, for himself, he has standards, however slight.

James can keep these standards as his own, and nobody else's, because he is really alone in the world. He is a billiard ball bouncing off people, not sticking close. As soon as he begins to form sexual alliances with other people, the two of them will need to negotiate joint rules of behavior. James's marriages never reached that point, and that is essentially why they did not have a chance. Sexuality is too basic, too urgent, and too emotional for a husband and wife to live together with different standards.

James's aloneness will never be the common pattern. "For this reason," Genesis 2:24 says, referring to Adam's passionate response to Eve, "a man will leave his father and mother and be united to his wife, and they will become one flesh." It's human nature: people will want to join their lives. They will not be satisfied with one-night stands; they will seek permanency. So they will have to wrestle with some joint standards—say, as a bare minimum, "honesty." People will also have children, and feel concern for their children's future. Through their children, the couple's sexual standards will radiate outward into the rest of society. Society is not a collection of individuals, but a web of individuals in relationship. This web requires sexual standards. If America seems to be an exception to this, it is probably merely because America is in transition.

Anthropologists have catalogued the sexual behavior of many different ethnic groups, and have found a bewildering variety of codes. They have not found, however, a people that has no code. Popular accounts of anthropology's findings about sex are often deceptive, too, in that they give tiny and disappearing tribal cultures equal weight to that of large and dynamic cultures. When you consider only large and enduring cultures, you find less diversity.

Anthropologist Nigel Davies writes, "Marriage is one aspect of tribal life that inevitably reappears in all advanced societies. . . . Marriage was invariably subject to strict control, designed to protect the family unit. The exceptions, or safety valves, such as wife-lending, merely proved the rule; almost everywhere plain adultery was taboo and punishable by death." Premarital sex is also strictly regulated in advanced societies, at least for women. "Premarital free love . . . has only become once more acceptable in the West in the past two decades, a curious instance of the readoption of an abandoned tribal custom."

In 1934 British anthropologist J. D. Unwin published an extensive study attempting to show that the development of culture was inevitably linked to the control of sex; the more careful the sexual regulation, the more developed the society, he claimed. Unwin's claims have fallen out of fashion, partly because the criteria for societal development are problematic. (Was the Athens of Plato developed or underdeveloped? What about the Berlin of Hitler? And what do we make of the fact that both societies were, by Christian standards, sexually immoral?) Nevertheless, it stands that all cultures have sexual rules, and that advanced civilizations protect marriage and family life with strict laws against adultery and premarital sex. If James wants to live without rules, he will have to go out of this world. In a sense, he already has: He is alone.

Flexible morality

Some people make subtler objections to sexual rules than James does. They would admit that sexual standards are necessary, but they hate to see these standards rigidly codified. That, they say, goes against the very nature of good and loving sexuality. Sex should be spontaneous and emotive. Let us honor principles such as love, care, and communication, they say, but not a rigid code.

Among American theologians, James Nelson is perhaps most influential in holding this position: "Sexual sin is alienation from our sexuality; harmful ideas and acts arise out of this. When I become alienated from my body and my sexuality, I will tend to see the world as though everything involves an either/or conflict. Everything will be either good or bad, right or wrong, gay or straight, me or them." Nelson would like us to be more flexible in our evaluations, looking at what people mean by their actions, and taking into account the entire picture of their lives. And he goes further: He says that the desire to categorize actions as right or wrong is itself a symptom of sinfulness, which he defines as alienation from our sexuality. He seems to be thinking of stereotypical "old maids": people so uncomfortable with their bodies they don't like paying attention to subtleties and inner meanings in sexual deeds. It is easier just to condemn it all as sin.

The Victorian preoccupation with rules has fed this critique. Andrew Greeley is surely right in claiming, "In its most rigid form, the past wisdom says, 'All will be well in your marriage if you are faithful to one another.' . . . The legalism of the past . . . assume[s] that the problems of sexuality can be solved in terms of whom you sleep with and what particular organs are combined in what ways."

That form of legalism is dead wrong. Sex can be "proper" without being at all "right." Many can sincerely say, as the rich young ruler did to Jesus, that they have obeyed the commandments; but despite keeping the sexual rules, they have wretched sexual lives. Every marriage counselor sees couples who have never committed adultery, but whose relationship seethes with anger, frustration, and bitterness. It is *not* enough that married couples be faithful to each other, if faithfulness merely means staying out of bed with other people.

However, staying out of other people's beds is not a bad place to start toward more positive forms of faithfulness. Most people instinctively mistrust someone who cannot or will not stay out of bed with other people. They should. He shows with his body that his love is not pure. He is going in two directions at once.

Rules cannot become the last word on sexuality. That is the sin of legalism. Yet rules, if they are not the last word, still must be spoken.

Two kinds of standards
There are two kinds of standards. Many of the most important are positive callings. "Love the Lord your God with all your heart and with all your soul and with all your strength and with all your mind" (Luke 10:27) is the greatest commandment, though there is a great deal of fuzziness in applying it, and no "penalty" for disobedience. The same could be said of "Honor your father and your mother." Such commands set an ideal. They confront us, they teach us, they rebuke us, but they can also be easily evaded by someone who imagines himself to be good, and who does not want to be contradicted.

Another kind of rule is more definite, and usually negative. These are the rules that people object to. "You shall not steal." "You shall not murder." "You shall not give false testimony against your neighbor." "You shall not make for yourself an idol." "You shall not commit adultery." Such standards are "yes or no," "right or wrong." James Nelson suggests that those alienated from the body will like such commands. The truth is nearer the opposite. These are commands suited to the body. The body is always definite. It either does, or does not, do a certain act. For Nelson, sexual acts are a form of communication, their meaning dependent on what you have in mind. But the physical body sets limits on such flexibility: theft is theft regardless of motive; someone else's bed is never to be confused with my bed, no matter how I yearned for "wholeness" while I was there.

Real morality requires both kinds of command. Rules cannot

probe the heart; they can keep you out of the wrong bed, but they cannot teach you how to make love in your own. Today, though, we live in a society that would like very much to retain only the positive commands—only to speak of meaningful relationships and love and wholeness. This is really an attempt to escape—to escape responsibility for our actions, to escape the body and its definiteness. We would like never to be "judged." We would like to be only what we imagine ourselves to be. The negative commands force us to confront the truth about ourselves.

So it happens repeatedly. A group of Christians builds a very powerful ideology of victory over sin. They are elated with their certainty that God has given them power over evil—until one of their leaders is caught in adultery, or with his hand in the till. Then there is no escaping the factuality of the sin—he did it with his body. Evidently that Christian group has not yet cornered the Holy Spirit. They had no doubt sinned against the positive standards a thousand times. But it was the negative standard—the rule—that caught their attention.

It is the same in secular communities. Journalists, for example, periodically build to a peak of self-congratulation for their disinterested objectivity—until it comes out that one of their respected peers invented a Pulitzer prize–winning story. Then journalistic self-certainty crashes down for a while.

To avoid such "right or wrong" morality is to evade the truth about ourselves, and to evade responsibility for repairing our wrongs. America is, sexually, in such a condition today. Much is wrong—AIDS, abortions, teenage pregnancies, broken families—and the victims are everywhere. But who is responsible? No one, but no one, steps forward to say, "We are."

No adultery

Biblical Christianity is hardly weighed down with sexual negatives. The handful in the Bible focus on a single proscription: no sex outside marriage. Two commands are central: no adultery, and no *porneia*. (*Porneia* used to be translated "fornication," but is now usually translated more generally as "sexual immorality.")

Negatives are uniformly hard to justify. (Try, for example, to justify the absolute "You shall not murder.") In my years of answering teenagers' questions about sex, I have been asked time and again on various topics, "What's wrong with it?" There is often no direct answer to that. Nothing is wrong with it except that it isn't right enough. It's off the mark. To understand the negative commands, you must study the positive values they are meant to protect.

Sexual rules function as boundary markers: sexual salvation is experienced within these lines. Living within the boundaries does not, I emphasize again, constitute a virtuous life. But negative rules define the field where virtue can operate with freedom and creativity, and not be stymied by impossible conditions.

Let me begin by considering the seventh commandment: You shall not commit adultery. It is, unquestionably, the most basic rule of biblical sexuality. While the Old Testament Israelites tolerated polygamy, and seemed (in the male-dominated patriarchal period) to take a lenient view of prostitution, they were absolute about adultery involving a married woman. Israel condemned both man and woman to death. Later, the church would eliminate the double standard by requiring the same fidelity of men that had always been required of women.

The rule against adultery is a fence around the institution of marriage. Or perhaps more accurately, it is a fence around the potentiality of Eden—that two people who are drawn together from aloneness to a shared life, becoming "one flesh," should have no sexual competition or interference.

Marriages are as different as people are different. They adopt many different styles. But all marriages, regardless of their style, originate with the same response that Adam made to Eve: passionate recognition of each other. "This is bone of my bone, and flesh of my flesh" (Gen. 2:23). In our society, we have institutionalized this urge in the conventions of dating and romance—a person must feel "in love" to marry. In other cultures, marriages may be arranged. (The Christian West insisted, very early on, that such marriage could not be forced on someone against his or her will.) Yet when the partners come together, they discover this passion to know and cling to each other. D. H. Lawrence wrote, "The instinct of fidelity is perhaps the deepest instinct in the great complex we call sex. Where there is real sex there is the underlying passion for fidelity."

The reflexes of love
So partners say: "Let us be together always. Let this love be for us

alone." And they ask, even if silently, for guarantees: "Never leave me. Promise there will never be someone else." Marriage, you might say, is an instinctive institution. Exclusivity and permanence are reflexes of love.

But—here is the problem—these reflexes do not stay. G. K. Chesterton wrote that polygamy is wrong because it is ungrateful. One woman ought to be enough to make a man spill over with joy for life. How petulant to wish for two! But polygamy, at least in the cultures I know, doesn't happen all at once. A man does not marry two women. He marries one woman—and then another, and another, usually with a spacing of years. A Kenyan psychiatrist, Samuel Gatere, told me that a second wife is often chosen at about the time we refer to as the "mid-life crisis." A man begins to feel old and has doubts about his virility, and he thinks his first wife cannot solve these difficulties because she, too, has aged. So he looks for another.

Passion cools; it cannot sustain itself without some outside help— and this help comes from our marriage vows. In Christian vows, we promise to love and receive love until death.

Sometimes people talk as though the commitments of marriage are at odds with the passion of romance. The old joke, "Marriage is a wonderful institution—but who wants to live in an institution?" carries on this tradition. But really, the commitments enable the charmed conditions of passion to achieve their natural goal. Philosopher Diogenes Allen writes,

"All of us have had moments . . . when falling in love, we seem to float on air. The whole world seems wonderful, and we take in our stride people who normally irritate us. . . . For a while we simply seem to be able to love anyone—to love our neighbor—without any effort at all.

"These momentary occasions can be simply that. But they can also give us a glimpse of what it would be to love our neighbor all the time. To that extent, such moments can be like little seeds, which, if planted and nurtured, can grow and affect our character. We can become less and less dominated by the need to be recognized by others and more able to pay proper attention to others." And he adds, "Romantic love not only gives us the goals God has for us in our own experience—to love well, always, and faithfully, goals which can be achieved only by the guidance and strength provided by ethical and religious commitment—but also helps us in the early stages of achieving it. What is easy and joyous introduces us to our task: to become always what we are not. We are to care for the beloved even when the task is no longer easy and effortless. . . ."

Allen points out that unqualified commitment is never made on strictly practical grounds. No one can be sure in advance that such a commitment will pay off in happiness. You commit yourself to a person, "for better or worse, richer or poorer, in sickness or in health," only because something beyond your immediate situation—your faith in God, your sense of "ought," or your response to the sheer beauty you see in your beloved—tells you that you must.

Bad sex drives out the good
Does this mean, however, that we need a rule against adultery? Isn't the commitment to love and be loved enough? If a couple tries hard to love each other, won't they succeed in "affair-proofing" their relationship?

To Maggie Scarf, an affair is virtual proof that something is wrong with the marriage. "The affair's very existence . . . indicate[s] that the intimacy in the couple's emotional system is out of balance. Someone is frightened about getting too close, or someone is overly frustrated—hungering for an intimacy that is lacking." She assumes that partners in a good relationship won't be tempted by adultery. Good sex will drive out the bad.

Yet reality is often just the opposite: bad sex drives out the good. No one seems invulnerable to sexual temptation, and an affair, however "meaningless," has the potential to ruin even the best marriage. Paul Pearsall, though he advertises the superiority of "super marital sex," comments that "One of the saddest paradoxes among the thousand couples [studied] was the fact that the persons you would assume to be the best of all spouses sometimes became involved outside the marriage. If not actually interacting sexually, they were at least flirting with the possibility." He suggests that this is because an attractive marriage partner will be attractive to others outside the marriage as well. The "best partners" suffer the worst temptations.

A mere decade ago, popular books claimed that an occasional affair could spice up a relationship. Now, thanks to the cruel instructions of experience, "open marriages" are understood to be those with the bottom falling out. Adultery has devastating consequences. Maggie Scarf describes a woman who had discovered her husband's infidelity: She "found herself standing in the middle of a department store with no idea why she had gone there or what she had intended to purchase. 'I felt as if the very floor I stood on was moving, waving, and buckling underneath me. It was as if I myself and the world around me were completely unreal.' "

Philip Blumstein and Pepper Schwartz, in their sociological study *American Couples*, found that "Husbands and wives who had had extramarital sex were more likely to break up, whether it happened at the beginning of the marriage or after many years."

Their comments are revealing: "It is widely believed that with a truly happy relationship, partners would not be 'driven' to non-monogamy. Another piece of folk wisdom is that partners go outside for sex when there is too little of it at home. We find that heterosexual couples who are monogamous [that is, who don't commit adultery] have neither more nor less sex than those who are not. . . . Monogamous and non-monogamous heterosexual men and women are on average equally pleased with their sex lives together. Another possibility exists: that partners are non-monogamous because they are fundamentally unhappy with the relationship. There is no evidence for this contention. Heterosexuals who have non-monogamous sex are on average as happy with their relationships as monogamous people. But they are *not* as certain that their relationships will last. . . . For most heterosexuals, non-monogamy is associated with less commitment to a future together."

Taking a positive vow of commitment and internalizing the negative rule against adultery are two sides of the same coin.

Blumstein and Schwartz also collected data on couples who were living together. Eighteen months after their initial interview, such "cohabitors" were between two and four times more likely than married couples to have dissolved their relationship. (Gay and lesbian couples were even less stable.) And not coincidentally, the chances of affairs for a cohabiting couple were nearly twice as great. (Gay and lesbian couples were even more prone to affairs.) The lack of commitment and the potentiality for affairs went together—as did the likelihood of breaking apart.

A partner's infidelity is more than just a disappointing choice to prefer another person (for a night, or longer) but a stab in the gut. It threatens any relationship, regardless of how loving. It is an action that cannot be mediated by good intentions. It betrays the partner who has entrusted life, body, and soul to another. It makes him or her into a sexual competitor.

Is there any such thing as a meaningless fling? The apostle Paul, in his comments about the inevitability of sex creating unity, even with a prostitute, would deny it. So would the vast majority of Americans, if they were talking about their spouse's infidelity. Blumstein and Schwartz tried to differentiate between a meaningful affair and a meaningless fling. But the people they asked made little of the distinction. Among wives, for example, 93 percent were threatened by a meaningful affair by their husbands, and 84 percent by a meaningless fling. For husbands, the distinction was even smaller. Only among gay couples was there a widespread assumption that meaningless sex was a possibility.

Marriage demands, positively, that we make a pledge to love for life. Negatively, it demands that we abhor adultery. To brush aside that rule, emphasizing the positive pledge without the negative command, is to kid yourself. Adultery destroys the possibilities of Eden.

Richard and Janis met at their church's high school youth group, not long after Richard moved to town at the age of 16. Janis was a year younger. On their first date they shared their philosophies of life, which included their feeling that they wanted to wait until marriage to have sex. (They were pleasantly surprised to discover their agreement.)

Three months into their relationship, Richard told Janis that he loved her. Janis said she loved him too, and stayed up until three in the morning writing in her diary. She thought that someday she would want a record of this day of days.

Six months into their relationship, after a miniature-golf date, they went beyond kissing in the car and began to stroke each other's bodies passionately, hungrily. They were both surprised to find that they didn't feel at all guilty. The next day, though, they talked it over and decided that it wasn't right for them to be petting.

But they did it, week after week. They tried and failed to stop. Soon they didn't care about stopping, except occasionally when they "got the guilts," as they put it. One night Richard asked Janis whether she had ever thought of making love with him. She said she thought of it all the time. For several weeks they talked it over. It seemed they would either have to break up or make love—the middle ground was too difficult. And neither one of them could remember, no matter how hard he or she tried, just what was wrong with making love.

Richard and Janis lead us to consider the second great sexual prohibition of the Bible: *porneia*. Why is premarital sex wrong? And is it wrong in all situations? Does God really intend to condemn what Richard and Janis are contemplating?

Richard and Janis are very typical of high school lovers. They are not promiscuous. They act as though they are already married, which indeed they have vague plans someday to be. They feel tremendous love for each other, love that is something more than infatuation since they have spent so many hours together and know each other well. They are still dependent on their parents, but they have experienced considerable independence in school and in summer and part-time jobs.

Both of them intended to wait for marriage, and they still hold marriage in high esteem. It is not practical for them to think about marrying now. But if it worked out that they eventually could marry, that would be wonderful. The problem is right now. It is very hard for them to be together so much, and love each other so deeply, and yet not have intercourse.

Why should they not? On a practical level, there are several reasons, particularly pregnancy and sexually transmitted disease. However, Richard and Janis could use birth control pills (though if they did they would be atypical high school lovers). Assuming that they are both telling the truth about their virginity, disease should not be an issue for them. These practical concerns are significant, but far from absolute.

Actually, in and of itself, sexual intercourse between two such students may have "nothing wrong with it." That is, they may experience no obvious harm—no suffocating guilt or evident psychological damage. According to most studies, at least half of American high school students engage in sexual intercourse by the time they graduate, and of these, most continue to be sexually active up until the time they marry, usually sometime in their twenties. Yet the fabric of American society has yet to disintegrate. It may well be that we are following the Roman empire downward into decline, but don't expect to impress Richard and Janis with that argument. They have plenty of friends who are sexually involved, and it doesn't seem to have ruined their lives. Richard and Janis are not guilty of adultery—neither is married. They are not violating their own or others' marital vows. What is wrong with what they want to do? The question is acute in our culture, when marriages are delayed, and when, by some accounts, puberty begins early. Some would argue that expecting chastity under such conditions is sheer fantasy. Others would argue that trying to enforce chastity leads to all kinds of psychological trauma and antisocial behavior.

Divorced people and single adults, who have become so numerous, pose a related question. They are presumably mature enough to deal with the risks of a sexual relationship. Why should they be deprived of sex?

I have already dealt with many of the practical results of premarital sex in the first chapter of this book. For society as a whole, and for many women in particular, it is disastrous. Here, though, I want to deal with the problem on a different level. After all, if the biblical prohibition of *porneia* applies at all, it is a claim on each individual, no matter how mature and strong he or she may be. The law is aimed at society, but no less at the individual, whom it should train in righteousness. What is so "right" about avoiding premarital sex?

Another way of asking that question is: What is protected within the boundary against "fornication"? Two ways of life: marriage and celibacy.

Protecting the future
Prohibiting *porneia* protects future marriages, first of all. Richard and Janis will probably someday want to marry. Yet marriage is a difficult task. We want Richard and Janis, if at all possible, to marry successfully. By "successful" we mean even more than "long-enduring." We want them to create a marriage that endures in loving, giving, and deeply appreciating each other's worth.

The logic of the law against *porneia* is that the best marriages are formed where two people come together sexually only with each other, within the bounds of marriage. They both enter their first marriage as virgins.

Why so? Why should sex before marriage have anything to do with sex after marriage? Why should sex with one partner have any carryover effect on sex with another partner? The answer lies in Paul's exegesis of "one flesh" in 1 Corinthians 6:12–20. According to Paul, something happens when two people come together sexually, something independent of their intentions or their state of mind. Sex has its own meaning. That meaning stays with you, even after you have forgotten the particulars of the sexual act (as someone may, after enough partners, quite forget how many he has been with).

What is this indelible meaning? "Do you not know that he who unites himself with a prostitute is one with her in body?" (1 Cor. 6:16). The meaning is that you become "one" with a person who is not properly yours. That unity stays with you. That *person* stays with you. If there is only one partner, the specific personality and body of that one will stay with you. If there are many, there will be a fairly faceless crowd with you. But whether one face or a crowd of faces, they will be with you. If and when you do marry, they will, in a sense, "meet" your spouse. Your spouse will want to know about them (or if not, will sacrifice the intimacy of knowing an important aspect of your life).

Paul is saying that a person who has had sex is different from someone who has not had sex. He is also saying, undoubtedly, that someone who has had sex with two people is different from someone who has had sex with one person. Further, he is saying that someone who has had sex under proper circumstances—within marriage— will be affected differently than a person who has had sex under improper circumstances.

Paul makes no mention of virginity. (The Bible does not often mention it, though in Old Testament Israel a woman was supposed to be able to demonstrate to her husband that she was virginal [Deut. 22:13-30].) Yet Paul's logic may be easier to understand if we apply it specifically to virginity. Virgins ought to be different from nonvirgins, by Paul's logic. So it has been taught, in all advanced societies, where virginity was valued at least in women. Today the value of virginity is disallowed, mainly out of reaction against the double standard. We have eliminated the double standard by letting women be as promiscuous as men, rather than by insisting men be as faithful as women. It is believed today that virginity means nothing but an orifice penetrated or unpenetrated.

The first time
Yet the cult of "the first time" suggests that people realize virginity

does make a difference. A much-reviewed book collected stories from dozens of celebrities of their "first time." Movies frequently celebrate an adolescent "first time." Imagine how those movies would portray a 35-year-old who had remained a virgin. In the contemporary sense, a virgin is different, all right—badly so. A virgin does not know what it's all about. A virgin is naïve, "out of it," unformed, inexperienced.

For our culture, those qualities are bad. For Paul, they would undoubtedly be good. It is good for unmarried people to be sexually unformed. A virgin is inexperienced, and that makes him or her radically open to being formed by the "first time" with a husband or wife. A virgin is ready to bond firmly to another person. A nonvirgin has already made, and broken, at least one bond, which makes the second bond harder to form.

A woman who has been with other men, or a man who has been with other women, will always be able to compare—compare the beauty of bodies, compare the varieties of sexual technique. The other bodies stay with you, when you have known them that way. Yet comparisons are deathly to love. The person who marries as a virgin will be incapable of comparisons.

What are we to make of anthropologists' reports? They tell of tribal societies where premarital sex is encouraged during an adolescent period of life. Later, when they come of age, these promiscuous adolescents form enduring marriages. Doesn't that suggest that premarital experimentation makes no difference to marriage?

There are some uncertainties about these reports, for they often describe a tribal pattern that is vanishing and cannot be easily verified. (It dismays anthropologists how quickly these people become relatively Victorian once missionaries arrive.) In some cases, anthropologists have had difficulty understanding why so few illegitimate children are produced by the promiscuity their informers describe.

Nonetheless, taken at face value the reports remind us that premarital sex does not automatically lead to a breakdown of marriage. In our own time, many individuals—perhaps most—who marry and stay married had sex before they were married.

Still, it is notable that of advanced civilizations, until our own, all valued premarital virginity in women even if not in men. Nigel Davies writes, "The domination of male over female, acquired by him as a form of property, made it imperative that brides and even secondary wives should be virgins. . . ." But why this imperative? Not, evidently, for sexual pleasure, since someone with sexual experience is widely believed to offer greater technical expertise. Instead, he values the virgin because he takes pleasure in having a woman who has known no one else. His sexism is repellent. But the value he appraises is a real value.

Virgins have a kind of shyness of body, because their bodies have been given to no one. The shyness may be nothing more than shyness. But it can also be a sign that the body is highly valued, a gift to be presented to one person only. Someone who marries as a virgin will have a singular vision of marriage, not as the best possible option among other sexual liaisons, but as the only one. As monotheists are bid to bow to one God only, so a virgin enters marriage to be joined to one person only, forever. A marriage formed this way has a different quality from one in which both partners have been joined to other bodies.

Advice for the sexually experienced

Very well, someone says. That may be good for virgins, but very few adults today are virgins. They have had sexual experiences in high school and college and beyond. Or they have been married and are now divorced. What is the value for them in staying away from sex after all that?

Furthermore, don't you make widows into second-rate partners? They aren't going to become virgins again.

Perhaps this is why the Bible makes little of virginity. When Paul wrote warning the Corinthians away from prostitutes, he did not specify that his instructions were for virgins. Indeed, there probably were not many in Corinth. Yet Paul does not treat nonvirgins as lost causes. He has a positive command as well as a negative one. Not only does he say, "Flee fornication," but "Honor God with your body" (1 Cor. 6:18, 20).

That is precisely what a widow has presumably done. In her marriage, in bed, she has honored God. Her nonvirginity may represent a positive sexual achievement, rather than a negative one. So for Paul, she is not a second-rate partner at all.

But what about those who have lost count of their extramarital liaisons? What difference could one more make to a person who has known many? A virgin is different from a nonvirgin. But how different is a man who has known five women from a man who has known six?

The difference may not be in the number of past partners, but in whether the man has stopped adding more—or has not stopped. That would make, at any rate, a difference in his relationship to God. A person who continues to pursue unmarried sex decides not to honor God with his body. He refuses to use his sexuality for the purpose it was intended. If his excuse is that it is "too late for him," it is because he refuses to believe himself forgiven and renewed in the image of God. He refuses to believe that God can change the likes of him.

Whether a person ultimately marries or remains celibate, he or she is to be filled with the Holy Spirit. Paul urged the Corinthians not to be united to prostitutes because he wanted them to live in unity with the Lord. He clearly thought that, unless they stopped *porneia*, they would be incapable of honoring God with their bodies.

The question of sex outside of marriage is often put this way: "Why deprive them?" One must ask in response, Deprive them of what? Of sex? But of what kind of sex, if it is outside of marriage? Do we deprive them of sex as a compulsive need? Sex as an abuse of themselves and others? Sex as a depersonalized, short-term round of biological stimulation? Deprive them of the chance to make their bodies known to others, and then to have them compared and rejected?

For unmarried people, too, bad sex drives out the good. When easy sex is available, many do not wait and work for sex within strong marriages. Commitments become a rarity, because people don't need them to gain sexual pleasure. By not depriving single people of bad sex, we may end up depriving them of good sex.

A Christian will answer the question about "deprivation" another way as well. Modern people assume that life without sex is always deprived, but that is not an assumption Christians can make, since our Lord himself was celibate. In at least one case, celibacy was the very opposite of deprivation. His was the richest life ever lived.

The critical difference of commitment
Janis and Richard would protest. "But we love each other!" They would want to know how their situation can be like the one Paul

addressed. Prostitution, they would agree, is ugly. (It is considered uglier in our day, probably, than in Paul's, when it was a legitimate and sometimes even an honored profession. During times and places in which "decent" women went without an education, prostitutes could be the most interesting women in town.) But their love is nothing like prostitution.

Does love make the unity of Janis and Richard acceptable in God's sight? Is love the critical variable? It does not seem so, in Paul's way of thinking—at least, not if love is merely an emotion. He does not mention love or lovelessness in his argument to the Corinthians. (People do sometimes love their prostitutes. Would this have made the difference for Paul?) He is concerned with the kind of unity that sex creates. With a prostitute, the unity is anti-God. When would it be pro-God? Paul does not say, but he undoubtedly knew what Jesus had taught: in marriage, sexual unity is God-ordained. Only marriage can offer a love like God's, unlimited by time or change. Marriage is defined, in fact, by the commitment to lifelong love.

Janis and Richard, no matter how much they love each other, cannot be sure that they will stay together. Statistically, the likelihood of teenagers staying together in a sexual relationship for even a year is very small. If love were the justification for their coming together sexually, what would justify coming apart? The loss of love? Then that is not the kind of love that interests God. He values a love that refuses to die.

What about the chance that Janis and Richard will someday marry? We can hope they will; but even if they did, that would hardly justify sexual relations now. Premarital sex makes a poor preparation for marriage. Paul Pearsall notes that in the 1,000 couples he studied, "the large majority of their problems originated during the bonding phase of their relationship.

"Typically, the sexual interaction was male-instigated and female-dictated.... There was little verbal communication during the sex of courtship, and the women reported rare or inconsistent orgasmic experience.... Couples fell into bad habits, rushing sex, using it for negotiation, feeling guilty, trying to sneak to have sex and all, and sometimes cheating on a partner for sex while staying with the courting partner for a relationship." Pearsall concludes, "Sexual intercourse between men and women is constructive only within marriage." He adds, "It is interesting to note that Masters and Johnson and other sex therapists almost always tell their couples in treatment to stop having intercourse, to become reacquainted on deeper and broader personal levels before moving on to the intimacy of sexual intercourse. I suggest that we use this recommendation for our courtship patterns as well. A little preventative sex therapy couldn't hurt."

What difference does a piece of paper make?

Commitment is what Richard and Janis lack. You cannot measure commitment, however, strictly by seeing whether there has been a wedding. For some people, a wedding ceremony is just a nod in the direction of tradition; they pledge their fidelity only "as long as we both shall love." You would hardly call sex in a movie star's sixth marriage less promiscuous than what Richard and Janis are contemplating.

A church ceremony never appears in the Bible, and if a couple prefers not to have one today, that does not in itself prove them uncommitted. Occasionally one hears of a couple who have been living together for thirty years. To all the world they appear married—except that, for reasons of their own, they never said "I do."

So what good is a wedding? Before I try to answer that, let me distinguish between three levels of premarital sex: recreational, experimental, and preceremonial.

Recreational sex is sex devoid of commitment. The two individuals come together for the pleasure of it. They may be open to a permanent bond but that is far from the front of their minds. They enjoy each other for the moment. Paul was talking about recreational sex when he wrote to the Corinthians.

Experimental sex also has no commitment, but it is interested in commitment. This is the most common form of premarital sex today. Temporary pleasure is not primarily what the two partners are after; they are after long-term love. They feel drawn to each other. However, they are not yet willing to commit themselves to each other.

Most couples who are living together fit this description. For them, "living together" is a trial period. They want to see how it feels to share life. Very, very few cohabiting couples stay in that state indefinitely. (Blumstein and Schwartz were unable to locate enough cohabitors who had been together ten years or more to make a statistical sample.) They either marry or they split. The majority split.

Thus far, surveys suggest that experimental sex does not improve marriages by weeding out incompatible couples. Couples who live together before marriage are more prone to divorce, not less. The apostle Paul's view of sex would make the effectiveness of trial marriages a moot point, anyway. Trial marriages are only useful if, in many cases, the trial fails—you find through living together that you aren't suited to each other. You can then walk away unscathed. But Paul would say you cannot walk away unscathed. Sex always creates a unity between two people, a unity that has lasting effects.

Preceremonial sex is between two people who believe they are committed. They intend to marry. They may simply get carried away before the wedding day. Or they may consider the actual ceremony a technicality. Once they have committed themselves to each other, they ask, "What difference does a piece of paper make?" Isn't the commitment what matters?

Donald Joy has pointed out that, from a pastoral point of view, we should treat preceremonial sex differently from recreational sex. The couple who gets carried away a week before the wedding are worlds apart from the couple who use each other's bodies for an evening's pleasure. We would want to break up the couple who were using each other; we would want to bring forgiveness and healing to the couple who got carried away. Joy argues, in fact, that biblical *porneia* refers only to degraded, depersonalized sex. Preceremonial sex is sin, he says, but it is a different and lesser sin—that of "defrauding one another—making the gestures of full trust without guaranteeing through social/legal protocol that such trust was indeed merited."

The problem is that in actual practice (as Joy makes clear) there is seldom a clear distinction between experimental sex and preceremonial sex. Among teenagers, for example, half the sexually active 15-year-old girls say they intend to marry their partners—though almost none do. Among single adults, too, sex is usually reserved for "serious" relationships—though most of these go nowhere. Many couples convince themselves that they are committed to each other, that marriage is around the corner. When they are in love, they believe fervently that nothing could break their commitment. However, when pressures build on them, or feelings change, they decide they are not so committed after all. Even formally engaged couples frequently break their engagements.

Private promises and public celebrations

In "preceremonial sex," we can see what difference a piece of paper makes. It is a way of separating serious commitment from wishful thinking. A piece of paper clarifies just where the couple really stands. Are the lovers really serious about committed love? Then why will they not demonstrate it to the community in a formal, legal celebration?

Richard and Janis would respond, "We would if we could, but we're not ready for marriage. We're too young." In that case, they are also too young for sex. Whatever keeps them from full, public commitment—age, finances, an uncertain future—should also keep them from uniting their lives sexually. If they are not ready for one, they are not ready for the other.

In times past, when no one escaped the view of the community, a marriage ceremony made less difference. It was often enough of a ceremony that two people moved in together. A man who deceived a woman—or vice versa—would have to answer for his behavior. That was clearly the situation in ancient Israel, which left no record of a marriage ceremony but obviously had committed marriages. When Isaac took Rebekah into his mother's tent, his action spoke as loudly as wedding vows. From then on, he had the obligations of a husband.

The situation today is radically different. Our society is too large and impersonal to observe commitments informally. It relies on legalities. Not so long ago you could buy a car with a handshake. You can't now, and for good reason: too many people don't follow through on their personal commitments. They may fully intend to pay for the car, but six months later when they are short of cash, they don't manage to pay the bill.

So we ask people, before they borrow money, to put their name on the line formally and legally. We want them to follow through on their commitments, and this is the best way we have of ensuring that they will. Not everybody needs the formality—some people actually are as good as their word—but in the interests of justice we make everybody do it. Should we take any less serious interest in seeing that people follow through on their commitments to love each other forever?

A couple needs all the support it can get. The marriage ceremony, with its celebrative vows before family, friends, and God, and its legal framework, obviously does not guarantee a relationship that endures, let alone one that grows in love. But it is a support and a protection. "Preceremonial sex" would count on private promises. Experience in our time has shown that private promises are as durable as morning dew.

Is abstinence possible?
Can Richard and Janis do it? If they are convinced that sex would be wrong at this time in their lives, will they be able to restrain their sexual desires?

My contact with teenagers has shown me that they can. Many do. But it is not easy, and the difficulty is not just in their biological makeup. Our society offers them almost every conceivable stimulation of sexual desire (from movies, TV, advertising, and radio), an ideology of sex that discourages abstinence, and an environment (the nearly absolute privacy of dating) that makes sex convenient and comfortable. These conditions are not inevitable. Other places and other times have organized courtship differently. (Chaperones, for example, would seem outrageous in modern America, but must that be the case?) So long as we ask Richard and Janis to oppose all the forces of modern American society singlehandedly, without help or support, we can count on a good number of failures. By no means all kids will become sexually involved. But many will.

Which brings us again to the role of rules. They cannot save, and we must be careful not to proclaim them as though they can. If we acted as though there were a gigantic difference between those who keep the rules and those who don't, between virgins and nonvirgins, we would make the rules out to be more than they are. Keeping the biblical rules does make a difference. But it does not make the difference between life and death, between saved and unsaved.

Rules are, at best, a cradle for virtue. At worst, they are a substitute for genuine salvation. Whether Richard and Janis give in to temptation, or whether they manage to control their desires, they will still need to experience God's forgiveness and grace.

Chapter 7

THE ETHICS OF
DESIRE

*M*artin Nestor has a secret so silly, so junior-highish, it makes him squirm with embarrassment. Two weeks from today he is due to speak at the Sweetwater Christian Conference. He has a conference brochure on his desk, and occasionally he looks at it to see a thumbnail-sized portrait of the reason for his agitation: Barbara Shinar, program director. Small as it is, the soft-focus, back-lighted photo catches the overspilling enthusiasm of Barbara's eyes.

Martin argues with himself about the excitement he feels. Part of him can't see any harm in the attraction of a wonderful woman. Barbara is an exciting, spiritually alive person. She has meant so much to him. Something would be wrong if he did not feel drawn to her. A part of his personhood, and hers, would be denied.

And yet he is disturbed by the intensity of his response. He has not felt such attraction for his wife in years. Martin is well aware of Jesus' warning that lust is equivalent to adultery. He has never been sure precisely how to apply those words because the attraction of women is so basic a part of the male makeup. He cannot imagine how to do away with it.

What could he do? Wear blinders? Cut off all relations with Barbara?

So far as Martin can see, so long as his responsibilities take him near her, he will feel this excitement.

In her best-selling book, *Nice Girls Do*, Irene Kassorla writes, "In order to have good sex, you *must* forget about the controls you were taught as a child concerning your genitals and your body. Adults are overly controlled children who need to be advised on how to relax, loosen up, and let go." She is saying what many people believe: that our problems (in life, but particularly in sex) come from repressing our feelings.

The modern view is that desire is normal, inevitable, and healthy. To stifle sexual feelings would go against nature. It is probably impossible—plug one leak and the pressures of desire will pop out somewhere else—and likely to turn you into an unnatural creature of hidden impulses and repressed sexuality. According to some, this is how truly strange sexual perversions are created. The desires that cannot surface normally surface in some secretive, guilt-ridden form.

Is anything wrong with Martin Nestor? Of course not! The human being responds mentally and physically to sexual stimuli, and this is entirely normal. For that matter, all desire—for success, for riches, for a nice car and beautiful clothes, as well as for sexual intimacy—is regarded as inevitable and innocent. Or so many would say.

Desire according to the New Testament

The New Testament takes a very different view. Desire (or lust, which is one translation of the Greek word *epithymia*) is sometimes seen positively, but far more often negatively. Not only did Jesus warn that sexual lust is equivalent to adultery. In the parable of the Sower, "desires for other things" are like thorns that grow up and choke the plants that grow from the seed of the Word. Jesus also warned that "uncleanness" comes from inside a person. "For from within, out of men's hearts, come evil thoughts, sexual immorality, theft, murder, adultery . . ." (Mark 7:21).

In Paul's theology, desire is the means by which the "flesh" —life alienated from God—expresses itself. *The New International Dictionary of New Testament Theology* describes it this way: "[Desire] urges man to activity. When all is said and done, it expresses the deeply rooted tendency in man to find the focus of his life in himself, to trust himself, and to love himself more than others. . . . The power of the 'old nature' (Eph. 4:22) is seen in *epithymia* [desire]."

According to Scripture, evil is not only in the satanic powers; it is in us. So our desires cannot be trusted. The association of desire with evil is very common in Paul's writings (see Gal. 5:16; Eph. 2:3; Rom. 6:12; 2 Tim. 3:6; Titus 3:3). The unsaved person is a prisoner of desire. The Christian (like Martin Nestor) may be. The things they desire—women, men, houses, riches—may not be wrong in themselves. But so long as desires express the person's will to please himself apart from God, the desires manifest sin. They are thorns growing up in the field. A thorn is a perfectly good plant by itself, but not in a place that was meant to grow wheat.

So what does the New Testament propose that we do with wrongful desires? What is Martin supposed to do about Barbara? The biblical solution is never self-control or suppression alone. Paul makes it quite clear that such a solution is unworkable, leading only to a destructive internal conflict. "We know that the law is spiritual; but I am unspiritual, sold as a slave to sin. I do not understand what I do. For what I want to do I do not do, but what I hate I do. . . . What a wretched man I am! Who will rescue me from this body of death?" (Rom. 7:14–15, 24).

The solution lies in a transformation through which the desires of the Spirit become the determining focus of life. "So I say, live by the Spirit, and you will not gratify the desires of the sinful nature. For the sinful nature desires what is contrary to the Spirit, and the Spirit what is contrary to the sinful nature" (Gal. 5:16–17).

The Spirit provides self-control as one of its fruits (Gal. 5:22), but self-control is secondary. The word occurs fairly rarely in Scripture. It is never an end in itself, but a tool for the Spirit to use. The lack of emphasis would be particularly striking in the culture to which Paul wrote. Greek philosophy gave great significance to self-control and moderation. They were the epitome of the virtuous life. A man was supposed to master himself. For Paul, God's Spirit was to master. The Spirit must renew our spirits with a new set of desires.

Can sex be controlled?
It is true that chastity has not, for males, often been an ideal in human history. Even in Christianized medieval Europe prostitution

was tolerated; theologians considered it the necessary cost of keeping young men from having sex with young women. (Men seldom married before their late twenties or early thirties—the difficulties of late marriages are not a recent phenomenon.)

Through the Reformation and Counter Reformation, however, and beginning even before, this situation changed. Brothels were closed down. Fornication was prosecuted in the courts. In some places, notably Italy, sodomy began to be attacked vigorously. Historians find that this societywide suppression of sexuality was quite successful. Lawrence Stone comments, "Despite the late age of marriage, bastardy rates and prenuptial conception rates in the 17th Century were surprisingly low; and homosexuality was largely confined, so far as the records go, to the nobility and courtiers in the major cities." He notes the common practice of "bundling" during courtship, in which a young man and woman shared a bed for the night. Yet there was little sex, since there were few pregnancies. "Where did the libido go? . . . We do not know, and probably never will."

Evidently it is possible to bottle up sexual desires. But sexual suppression is not, as I have noted, the solution offered by the Bible. There must be a transformation through the Spirit, by which a new set of desires take control.

The way Paul applies this in 1 Corinthians 7 is illuminating. Sexual desires are not necessarily evil for Paul. He wants married people to have sex together as often as either wants to, to *satisfy* desire and *prevent* sin. Similarly, for an unmarried person who lacks self-control, he says that marriage is an appropriate solution. Paul's answer to illegitimate desire is a legitimate desire—the desire for sex with a husband or wife.

However, Paul suggests another solution, preferable to him. He recommends celibacy for those who have enough self-control to manage it. (He obviously thinks many people do.) For these people, Paul emphasizes the positive opportunity to be "concerned about the Lord's affairs—how he can please the Lord" and "to be devoted to the Lord in both body and spirit" in "undivided devotion to the Lord" (1 Cor. 7:32–35). In other words, the desires of the Spirit for Christian worship and service would dominate.

While "just say no" strategies may be somewhat effective, the biblical pattern is more accurately "just say yes"—yes to some person, some ideal, some work that the Spirit has given. The strategy of substituting the Spirit's desire for the flesh's desire has broad application. A young person may control his sexual desires through his greater desire for a godly marriage. A widowed or divorced person may control her desires through a greater desire for purity and single-mindedness.

For a Martin Nestor, cutting off relations with Barbara, or some other strategy of suppression, should be at best secondary. Martin Nestor needs to renew his desire for the things of the Spirit— including the woman to whom God has united him in marriage. "So I say, live by the Spirit, and you will not gratify the desires of the sinful nature" (Gal. 5:16). Sexual desire is not in itself wrong. But then, sexual desire is not, for Martin, "in itself." It is desire for a particular person—desire to have her in a way that has not been given by God. Such desire is impure, not because it is "in itself" dirty, but because it focuses Martin—and perhaps Barbara as well— on purposes that are not from the Spirit. When Martin is filled with the Spirit, these desires will not seem so dominant. He will be able to put them in their place, while others rise to preeminence.

Of course, this makes it sound very easy. Anyone who has dealt with sin knows that it is not. Life in the Spirit is not religious cruise control. It is warfare.

Until he was in high school, Gary had no label to put on his condition. He merely knew, with intense discomfort, that he was different from other boys his age. He heard them talking about girls, but girls didn't sexually attract him. Other boys did.

In high school, during Easter break, he went with his family to the beach and one day fell into conversation with two young gay men. They guessed that he was oriented toward homosexuality, and they acted very friendly—almost fatherly—to him. They explained what the gay lifestyle was all about. That was the first time Gary had heard of it. He was horrified and left them hurriedly. But he could not stop thinking about what they had said. He lay awake all night; he masturbated to fantasies of the two men. The next day he went back to try to find them, but they had gone.

Gary went back to high school more aware than ever of his secret. He was determined to keep it to himself. The news, he was sure, would be too much for his parents to take. He would face unthinkable persecution at school.

Yet Gary began to dream of a world in which he would not have to live in secret. The gay lifestyle the two men had described appealed not simply because of the possibility of sexual pleasure, but because of the possibility of living openly as what he felt he was condemned to be—yet being accepted, understood, not condemned.

Often Christians explain their rules against extramarital sex by saying that God wants only the best for his people, and the best is experienced in marriage. Yet homosexuals feel no desire for that best. They are not stirred by the opposite sex, but by their own sex. Homosexuals who try to marry out of hope that marriage will "cure" them often make disastrous marriage partners. So the question is: If God wants the best for everybody, isn't it a different best for these people? Shouldn't their best be with those they truly desire?

Over the years many people who are attracted to their own sex have written to me. Friends, too, have told me of their homosexuality. I know people who grew up like Gary. I cannot think of any group of Americans who suffer more than they do—often from persecution, but also from a terrible self-loathing when they discover desires in themselves that they wish were not there. In most high schools in America, there has been no "gay liberation." Those suspected of homosexuality can be treated by their peers in a way that human beings should never be treated.

We do not have to sympathize with the gay movement to empathize with the human beings in it. They insist—and I know of no reason to doubt their word—that they never chose their orientation. In fact, most would have given anything, at one point in their lives, to change their desires. Failing that, they must either remain celibate and secretive, or else act on their desires and endure the (at best) uneasiness and (at worst) persecution of society. Nobody would envy such choices.

If desire is natural

The gay movement is a logical result of the modern belief that desire—all desire, and particularly sexual desire—is natural, unchangeable, healthy. If that is so, then there is nothing wrong with homosexuals. They are merely different.

Yet, as we have seen, Jesus did not treat desire—heterosexual or homosexual or any other kind—as purely natural. The thorns that grow up to choke the good plants are desires. Paul's theology treats desire as the normal means for "the flesh"—life out of relationship with God—to express itself. Christians can never presume that a desire—any desire, whether for sex or possessions or glory—is normal and naturally good. The "natural man" as we know him is out of kilter with his true created nature. Every desire must be tested by the Spirit.

The Spirit speaks through Scripture, and from it we learn that homosexual desires lead to sin. They are an indication to Paul, as he examines the gentile world, that a fundamental rebellion against God undergirds that culture. They had "exchanged the glory of the immortal God for images made to look like mortal man and birds and animals and reptiles," and "exchanged the truth of God for a lie." As a result, "God gave them over to shameful lusts. Even their women exchanged natural relations for unnatural ones. In the same way the men also abandoned natural relations with women and were inflamed with lust for one another" (Rom. 1:22–27).

It is important to keep this in perspective. Scripture has little to say about homosexual acts, and apart from this passage, nothing to say about homosexual desires. Certainly whenever homosexuality is mentioned, usually in a list of sins, it is treated in a thoroughly negative way. Since Paul regarded sexual sin as uniquely damaging, we can understand why. Yet homosexuality apparently concerned the New Testament writers (who lived close to it) less than it concerns many modern Christians.

In Romans 1, Paul's topic is not homosexuality. He is writing about the universality of sin, probably raising homosexuality as an issue precisely because he wants to catch pious Jews in his trap—for having waxed eloquent on homosexual sin, he moves quickly to this sentence: "You, therefore, have no excuse, you who pass judgment on someone else, for at whatever point you judge the other, you are condemning yourself, because you who pass judgment do the same things" (Rom. 2:1). He does not mean that all are homosexually involved, but that all are equally guilty of sins, which he has listed to include greed, envy, gossip, arrogance, and boasting. In the same horrified tone with which the pious Jews condemn homosexuals, they themselves deserve condemnation. "There is no one righteous, not even one; there is no one who understands, no one who seeks God" (Rom. 3:10–11). No one who reads Romans 1 in context can find any grounds for comparing himself favorably with homosexuals.

A new situation
Homosexual behavior has been known in many—some say all—cultures. In very few of these cultures has it been approved; most developed civilizations have regarded homosexual behavior unfavorably, and the first laws against it were passed in Mesopotamia four thousand years ago. But rarely have societies appeared powerfully motivated to punish homosexual behavior either. In some tribal societies, a group of people had a special status that included homosexuality; they were not usually ordinary citizens, but held a unique role in the rituals of that society, as (for example) transvestites and shamans.

Perhaps the most famous example of a society that sanctioned homosexual behavior was classical Greece, where relations between men and young boys were admired as the highest form of love. Michel Foucault makes the point that the inevitable instability, brevity, and nonreciprocity of these relationships troubled the ancient Greeks; their anxiety led them increasingly to spiritualize and desexualize the relationship. Nevertheless, the claim is often made, and with some legitimacy, that the modern gay movement is rooted in the classic heritage of Plato and Aristotle.

But our situation is quite different from that of ancient Greece, and indeed, different from any before in history. What is new is not homosexual behavior, or even the openness of homosexuals. What is quite new is a generation of men and women who say their desires are exclusively or primarily homosexual. They are not transvestites, nor do they have a special role in society; they are ordinary men and women.

Psychologist Stanton Jones summarizes the evidence this way: "While homosexual behavior seems to exist in all societies, the concept of homosexual orientation as a lifelong and stable pattern does not, and is in fact rare in preindustrial societies...." Michel Foucault makes the interesting point that the idea of a constitutional homosexual orientation came first to doctors in the Victorian era, who shifted the discussion from sexual *actions* to sexual *perversions*. "As defined by the ancient civil or canonical codes, sodomy was a category of forbidden acts.... The nineteenth-century homosexual became a personage, a past, a case history, and a childhood....

Nothing that went into his total composition was unaffected by his sexuality. It was everywhere present in him: at the root of all his actions.... The sodomite had been a temporary aberration; the homosexual was now a species."

Since Victorian times we have thought of homosexuals as a category of people. Has this categorization, or some other factor of modern society (perhaps the breakdown of families), made men and women into constitutional homosexuals? Or were constitutional homosexuals always present, but unrecognized? I do not think anyone knows. In ancient Greece, where no stigma was attached to homosexual behavior, every man was considered bisexual—except that the Greeks would never have invented such a term, since their mindset approached sexuality from the standpoint of pleasure, and you could have pleasure with any creature that could apply friction to your genitals.

A misunderstanding of Romans 1

So we are dealing with a new situation, nonexistent or unrecognized in biblical times: Some men and women desire sexual relations only within their own gender. Since this is a new situation, does the Bible speak to it? A reading of Romans 1 is widely used by homosexual apologists who want to remain within their Christian heritage. They say the Bible in general, and Romans 1 in particular, condemns homosexual pederasty and prostitution, not loving sexual relations between consenting adults who are constitutionally homosexual. Romans 1 in particular speaks of women and men who "exchanged" natural relations for unnatural relations. According to this interpretation, Romans 1 must be treating heterosexuals who perversely chose to behave homosexually. It cannot deal with constitutional homosexuality at all, since true homosexuals never "exchanged" one desire for another.

Sometimes this position uses contradictory logic. Some who cite the historical prevalence of homosexuality as proof that it is normal, in the same breath claim that biblical condemnations of such homosexuality have nothing to do with our situation. You can't have it both ways. If the condemnations are irrelevant to our situation, so is the prevalence of what they condemned.

In any case, the claim (made by the influential historian John Boswell, and followed by some evangelicals) that Romans 1 deals with the perversity of heterosexuals or bisexuals, not constitutional homosexuals, is badly flawed scriptural interpretation.

Richard Hays of Yale Divinity School, in an article published in the *Journal of Religious Ethics*, writes, "Boswell's remarks presuppose that Paul is describing some specifiable group of heterosexually-oriented individuals whose personal life pilgrimage has led them beyond heterosexual activity into promiscuous homosexual behavior.... Paul has no such thing in mind. He is not presenting biographical sketches of individual pagans; he is offering an apocalyptic 'long view' which indicts fallen humanity as a whole. Certainly Paul does not think that each and every pagan Gentile has made a personal decision at some point in his or her individual history to renounce the God of Israel and to worship idols instead! The 'exchange' of truth for a lie to which Paul refers in Romans 1:18–25 is a mythico-historical event in which the whole pagan world is implicated.

"... In the same way, the charge that these fallen humans have 'exchanged natural relations for unnatural' means nothing more nor less than that human beings, created for heterosexual companionship as the Genesis story bears witness, have distorted even so basic a truth as their sexual identity by rejecting the male and female roles which are 'naturally' theirs in God's created order. The charge is a corporate indictment of pagan society, not a narrative about the 'rake's progress' of particular individuals. Boswell's misinterpretation of this passage shares with much of the history of Western interpretation of Paul an unfortunate tendency to suppose that Paul is primarily concerned with developing a soteriological account of the fate of individuals before God."

Was Paul correct?

Paul was indicting neither constitutional homosexuality nor heterosexual perversion, but homosexuality, period. You cannot very well look in his words for a distinction that was first made 1,800 years later. The real question is not what Paul thought of homosexuality, but whether, in the light of modern knowledge, he was correct. James Nelson writes, "Our ancestors-in-faith did not know what we now know about homosexuality as a psychosexual orientation, nor can we blame them for being persons of their own historical time." Is homosexuality truly "against nature" when studies find it in so many different societies? When Kinsey's studies found so many Americans who practice it? Can it be "against nature" when, as we now know, many homosexuals feel that *heterosexual* behavior would go against their nature?

One might question whether we know so much more about homosexuality than our ancestors-in-faith. Paul certainly had ample opportunity to observe homosexual behavior in the cities of the Mediterranean, where homosexuality was considered quite natural except by Jews and Christians. Perhaps he saw things differently simply because he had a different point of view.

How do we go about deciding what is natural or unnatural? Most of us judge by the way it makes us feel, or by our knowledge of what behavior is common. Modern knowledge about homosexuality comes from surveys and interviews, which establish people's experiences and feelings. But these sources are of very limited value if we share Paul's view that all humanity is constitutionally in rebellion against God. People born in sin will not necessarily feel its unnaturalness. And, as Stanton Jones notes, "Many behaviors judged to be sinful are cross-culturally robust; for example, crime."

Paul's idea of "natural" has nothing to do with cross-cultural observations or personal feelings. Hays writes, "Paul, if confronted by a study demonstrating that (say) ten percent of the population favor sexual partners of the same gender, would no doubt regard it as corroborative evidence for his proclamation that the wrath of God is being made manifest in rampant human unrighteousness." Paul's source of "natural" and "unnatural" is rooted in God's revelation, particularly in the Genesis account of the sexual love of Adam and Eve. This can be juxtaposed and compared with contemporary ideas about what is natural, but neither source of revelation is able to disprove the other, because each springs from utterly different premises. In the end, one must choose which source— Scripture, or contemporary experience—to trust.

Cruelty

Some complain that Paul was uninformed. Others complain that his message is cruel if applied to modern homosexuals. How can you tell someone that it is always wrong, under all circumstances, to act on his or her sexual urges? John H. McNeill writes, "Only a sadistic God would create hundreds of thousands of humans to be inherently homosexual and then deny them the right to sexual intimacy."

As we have seen, however, Scripture never regards desire as any kind of self-justification. On the contrary, the desires of a fallen humanity are dangerous. To live spiritually, many must stymie their desires—or more accurately, must allow their desires to be subordinated to the desires of the Spirit.

Suppose McNeill were referring to the common (and fundamental) desire to exert your power over other people. Is Jesus' Sermon on the Mount, therefore, sadistic because he told people to turn the other cheek, and to love their enemies? How is it that sexual desire has become the one drive that can never be contradicted? Any Christian confronts, in many areas, his constitutional predisposition to want what he should not have. If, as McNeill writes, only a sadistic God would allow people to be born with powerful desires that are wrong to fulfill, then God is a sadist regardless of what one thinks of homosexuality.

But God is no sadist. Sometimes he inflicts pain, but he does it from love. Scripture presents him as a God who understands our desires—understands them so well he knows they can easily lead us to death. When he contradicts our desires, it is because he wants to replace them with better desires.

What's wrong with it?
"The Bible says" is not a very satisfying answer for people raised on Enlightenment faith in reason. They want a reasonable explanation of why the Bible says homosexuality is wrong. But this the Bible does not offer, perhaps because it does not say very much about homosexuality at all.

From what we know about the Bible's idea of sexuality, however, we can suggest some reasons why homosexuality fails to live up to the Bible's ideals. Homosexual liaisons match like with like, whereas marriage creates the diversity-in-union of male and female. Marriages, which are meant to be a sign of God's kingdom, can reflect the full diversity of the human community in which God displays his image. ("In the image of God he created [humankind]; male and female he created them" [Gen. 1:27].)

The union of male and female may make a very practical difference, too. Blumstein and Schwartz, in their extensive study of American couples, noted that "The only couples who adopt non-monogamy as a way of life are the gay men."

"Many gay men," they commented, "do not care if their partners are monogamous. If a gay man is monogamous, he is such a rare phenomenon, he may have difficulty making himself believed." Unlike heterosexual couples, male homosexual couples who did stay together became decreasingly erotic together; sex with other partners was taking the balance of their erotic energy. Many other studies show similar results.

Female homosexual (lesbian) couples have been much less studied. They seem to be much less promiscuous than males, but their relationships are often plagued by misunderstandings and jealousies, and tend toward instability, according to Blumstein and Schwartz's data.

Instability among male homosexuals is apparently not due to a lack of interest in lasting relationships. Both men and women homosexuals often idealize a stable, monogamous relationship. J. R. Ackerley, describing his unsuccessful lifelong search for a permanent partner, wrote, "Though two or three hundred young men were to pass through my hands in the course of years, I did not consider myself promiscuous but monogamous, it was all a run of bad luck."

Some gay advocates argue that were it not for the oppressive influence of our society, homosexual relationships would endure. Perhaps so, but that remains a highly theoretical possibility. In gay communities in San Francisco and New York, where homosexuals can live without notable persecution, promiscuity seems to be higher, not lower.

The Bible, in its description of the roots of marriage, contains at least a hint of the reason for the instability of homosexual relationships: "For this reason [that is, because of the attraction of the woman] a man will leave his father and mother and be united to his wife, and they will become one flesh" (Gen. 2:24). The lasting, intimate bond we call marriage comes from a spontaneous response to the opposite sex. Could Adam have had the same surprised reaction to another man, and if he had, would it have led to a permanent bond? One can imagine that it might, but one can also imagine that it might not. Perhaps the strong bond of marriage, seen in all cultures, simply does not occur between members of the same sex.

As we have seen, this bond of love is meant to be a sign of God's kingdom. It shows forth the nature of God's love. Does a homosexual love? Certainly the homosexual intimacy we know at this point in time does not offer the faithful, singular love that cannot and should not be broken. As with all promiscuous or unstable liaisons, it offers pleasure to the young and beautiful at the cost of the old and less attractive. It easily turns exploitative. It does not offer the sustaining grace of lasting love, and so is not an image of the love of God for his people. From a non-Christian standpoint, there may be "nothing wrong with it." Homosexual relationships are not necessarily exploitative, shallow, abusive, or degrading. But from a Christian standpoint, there is not enough good in it. It does not show the glory of God's love.

The possibility of change

I know that this theological analysis will seem heartless to some, particularly those who feel that they are constitutionally, irredeemably homosexual in their desires. What are they supposed to do? They may not like the gay scene. But its sexual attraction is very powerful. So is the climate of acceptance it offers. Should they bottle up their sexuality and throw it in the sea?

I have seen too much of the misery inflicted on such people when they are simply condemned for wanting what they cannot help wanting. We must have something positive to offer them. As I have said, a Christian does not deal with sinful desires primarily by suppressing them. He allows the Spirit to renew his life with a new and better set of desires.

Some people say that homosexuals can change their orientation. Christian groups and therapists (as well as some non-Christian groups and therapists) work with homosexuals to help them transform their desires from homosexual to heterosexual. Their work is a highly controversial subject, with strong opinions voiced against it. The controversy is over the possibility of change. It is certainly true that many homosexuals have gone to extraordinary lengths, trying to change their desires through prayer, therapy, even electric shocks, and have been unable to change. Some speak with ferocity about the false claims they feel are made in advertising the possibility of change.

Others, however, say that they have changed. I have spoken at length to men and women who have left years in a homosexual lifestyle and are now married with children. They have impressed me as realistic and sincere. They almost always speak of the change as a gradual, difficult process, but they are quite clear that it is also thorough and deep.

Both groups tend to suspect the other. Those who have not changed are suspected of not truly wanting to change; those who have changed are accused of not being truly homosexual in the first place, or else of pretending to have changed when their desires and temptations really have not. The fact that someone has married does not settle the argument, of course. The individual might still be seething with homosexual desire. No one can see into another person and be sure of how much his desires have changed. Nor can someone see into another person and know whether he "really wanted to change."

Stanton Jones, an academic clinical psychologist who has studied the research literature, writes that the evidence is clear: "Change is possible for some. Every study done reports some successes. Some (Bieber, 1976) report about 33 percent success rate for conversion to heterosexuality. Masters and Johnson reported a 50–60 percent cure or improvement rate. In a curious logical *non sequitur*, gay activists use the statistics about modest cure rates to argue that no cure is possible."

Nature or nurture?
The argument over what causes homosexuality is related to this controversy. If genes or prenatal hormones cause it, presumably no change is possible. If homosexuality is learned from societal influences, it should be possible, at least in principle, to change. But research has not settled this issue. The latest reports suggest that prenatal, hormonal, or genetic differences may predispose some people toward homosexual desires, but do not in themselves "fix" an individual in any particular direction. A homosexual identity, however predisposed, probably develops from experiences in early family life or, maybe, during adolescence. Researchers are still uncertain as to how much influence social experiences have.

Whatever the cause of homosexuality, it is clear that the desire for one's own sex is deep-seated, not easily changed or removed through a simple set of procedures or one healing prayer. A person's sexual identity and sexual desires are very deeply a part of who he or she is.

Even relatively superficial desires—the erotic fascination of nine-teenth-century Chinese for tiny, maimed feet, or the modern Ameri-can sexual preference for undernourished bodies—would be difficult to transform. (Not that such erotic attractions are parallel to homo-sexuality; but they do suggest how difficult it is to alter sexual desire.)

Some homosexuals do change, and the judgment of Scripture on homosexuality suggests that all homosexuality must be trans-formed at some time in the course of salvation. The question is when. In the day of the Lord's coming? Or now? The healing of diseases poses an identical question. Knowing that God wants to heal, we still do not know when he will heal a particular disease. All we can do is ask him to do it, and persist in asking, and cooperate in the attempt to heal (whether with doctors or therapists or other healers).

But there is another positive possibility for homosexuals: They can be celibate. For their homosexual desires they can substitute the desires of the Spirit that Paul recommends in 1 Corinthians 7: "to be devoted to the Lord in both body and spirit" as people who abstain from sexual relations.

People react to this suggestion with horror. This is a positive possibility? Sexual pleasure is treated almost as a god in our time, and certainly as a nonnegotiable right.

Yet life does not really work out that way for everybody. Most people must be celibate for a large part of their lives, and a good many for all of their lives. The average widow, for instance, will be celibate for 11 years after her husband dies. Women who are divorced will be celibate much longer. Are their lives, or the lives of other celibate people, necessarily a horror?

Of course not. In reality, celibacy can be lived with grace and joy. I know quite well, for instance, widows who have been alone for as much as three decades after a life of active sexuality in marriage. I am sure it has not always been easy, but in their lives it is clearly gracious.

Perhaps one reason is that, unlike a homosexual's, a widow's situation is understood. She can be relatively open about her strug-gles without fearing that she will be ostracized. The church and community will support and encourage her in her difficulties, not stigmatize her because she has them. If Christians are ever going to provide a hopeful environment for homosexuals, the same kind of openness and support will be necessary. It is simply nonexistent today in most American communities.

We will need also to recover the high status that Christians historically, following the Bible, have given to celibacy. Celibacy is, like marriage, a sign of the kingdom. At least it may be so.

Chapter 8

CELIBACY AND MARRIAGE—SIGNS OF THE KINGDOM

*J*udy fell in love in college. She met Joe in a dorm lounge. They talked about football, ate some pizza, and afterwards went up to her room. "When I looked in the mirror, I had a wild look in my eyes."

After their graduation, Joe went to South America with three of his mountaineering friends. They were to climb some remote Andean peaks. Joe called Judy from a small city high in the mountains. He told her that he loved her and missed her. Judy said the same. Joe's voice was clear, as though he were just across town. When he finally hung up Judy cried for almost an hour.

Later she regarded that as a premonition. After three weeks of no communication she grew worried, and called other friends and relatives of the four. None of them had heard, either. The U.S. embassy in Lima could give no news. Judy and two other friends traveled to Peru, but could find no trace of the climbers. They had disappeared. The area they had hiked into was notorious for its bandits.

A year went by before hope thoroughly died. For two more years after that, Judy mourned. When she finally began feeling as though she could function again, she poured herself into her job. She had trained as a *teacher, and during the nine months of school her class of sixth graders took all her energy. Over the summer she lived a quiet life, keeping busy as a volunteer and sometimes traveling with a friend. She remained a dedicated football fan. Sometimes she fantasized that Joe would surface and would want a complete accounting of how the Raiders had done.*

She was sometimes lonely and wished for a man, but something kept her from opening herself to that. She found it easier to imagine continuing in her life alone than to imagine being with someone. Just thinking of meeting men and going out on dates tired her. She did not want to be held up to evaluation that way, and she did not want to evaluate others that way. If she was going to fall in love again, she told herself, it would have to be as miraculously as the first time. She knew that such miracles became less likely with every year. Her mother fretted at her that she ought to be out meeting some men, and she didn't mind her mother saying so. Yet she knew she wasn't going to do it.

When evangelical Christians write about sex, they usually concentrate on the joys and dilemmas of marriage. How can marriages be divorce-proofed? How can they be happy? The dilemmas and possibilities of single life are often ignored, or treated as a secondary issue—on the level with sex for handicapped people.

Yet today most people live a long period of adult life before marriage, and many never marry. Increasing divorce adds another large group to the singles population. The elderly, who are growing in number, add more, since a high proportion have lost a spouse. All of these groups, in addition to a sizable group of people whose desires are primarily homosexual, call us to offer a view of sexuality that applies to singles just as much as to married people.

For marrieds, it seems natural to pity the single person—to think of him or her as miserable and lonely, incomplete and "making the best of things." Just as sexual swingers idealize the ecstasy of intercourse, so conservative Christians idealize marriage. They want so much for single people to find the joy of a good marriage and begin really living.

This view of single sexuality is a far cry from the New Testament's.

Equals in the kingdom

God is in the process of redeeming all the world through his Son, and his work applies equally to the single and the married. Their salvation is not in being married, nor in being single. It is a salvation that breaks into their circumstances, whatever they are, transforming them. Of course, single people experience salvation in a distinctive way. But it is not an inferior way. Our temptation ought to be, in fact, to call their way superior. (That was certainly the temptation of Paul, and many of the church fathers.) The single person's way is closer to that of Jesus, who is the ground of our salvation.

Imagine, if you can, patronizing Jesus as a single person. "Why haven't you ever married?" he is asked. "You seem like such a nice person. I have a cousin in Bethsaida I'd really like you to meet."

When I imagine such a ludicrous scene, I realize how Jesus transforms ordinary expectations. Matters that seem quite important become embarrassingly flimsy when we encounter him. Our dreams and ambitions, our worries and fears are held up to his light, and most of them become quite transparent. "You are worried that you might end up miserably single? Come unto me, all you who are weary and heavily burdened, and I will give you rest. For my yoke is easy, and my burden is light." He offers single people a far greater joy than marriage can provide. He calls them, as he calls married people, to follow him.

What would Jesus say to Judy? Would he echo her mother's advice that she ought to get out and meet some men? Perhaps. Far more certainly, he would invite her—no, *call* her—to be his disciple now, as a single person.

Radicals and stewards

I owe a debt to my brother, William Stafford (a church historian), for helping me see that there have been two great patterns of response to Jesus' call to discipleship. One is the response of stewardship. The other is the response of radicalism.

If you give a steward a million dollars, he will invest it wisely and honestly, and use the profit for God's kingdom. The radical will immediately give it all to the poor. The steward, if he is an accountant, will try to witness to God by being an honest and hard-working accountant. The radical may be an accountant in order to pay the rent, but his heart will be in what he does after work. The steward will serve on the city council; the radical will demonstrate outside the doors. The steward works with the conditions of life as he finds them; the radical seeks fundamental change. The steward sees the necessity of compromise; the radical sees the necessity of purity.

In sexuality, the response of stewardship is marriage. One thinks immediately of Martin Luther. He had spent most of his life as a monk, earnestly climbing rungs on the ladder to heaven. He concluded that there was no ladder: God saves us without regard to our religious efforts. That included the whole monastic affair, and celibacy as part of it. Luther had practiced celibacy, yet concluded that celibacy could only be lived by "peculiar" persons, perhaps one in a thousand. Calvin had a better-balanced view, more in accord with Scripture. But it is Luther's ideas about sexuality that have become ours.

The steward knows that the business of caring for a spouse, raising children, and supporting a family will often make his life look very similar to that of his non-Christian neighbors. After all, making love with your spouse, changing your baby's diapers, and coaching your son's Little League team are not distinctively Christian tasks. But the Christian steward intends to do these ordinary tasks prayerfully and selflessly. He hopes to be a better parent, spouse, nurturer, and provider because of his faith.

The steward's response is completely familiar to most of us since it has totally dominated Protestantism. And it has come to almost equal prominence in Catholicism. In the Roman church, the celibate priesthood seems increasingly an anachronism. A great many American Catholics would gladly rid themselves of it.

Isn't Jesus the norm?

The steward assumes that marriage is the normal way to live; celibacy or singleness is a "peculiar" or unusual situation. But the radical answers this with a question: From where do we get our norms? From an observation of what is usual in the world as it exists? Or from the kingdom as it breaks into the world? Isn't Jesus our norm? Aren't we to follow in his steps?

The radical is not terribly interested in preserving and hallowing the world as it exists. He is focused on the coming kingdom. He sees the practical demands of ordinary life as an interference: He would rather serve God only. Not only is Jesus his model, so is Paul. In both he sees an active, dedicated life, in which no practical matter—finances, family needs, political realism—is allowed to interfere with the cause of God's kingdom.

Celibacy is only one aspect of a life radically devoted to God. The radical may also, in imitation of Christ, favor a simple lifestyle, unencumbered by the responsibilities of possessions. He may eschew the right to defend himself, turning the other cheek. Often, he will give up his own individual freedom, choosing to work as part of a dedicated cadre. Thus, the traditional monastic vows were poverty, chastity, and obedience.

For the radical, celibacy is not so much a sacrifice as an opportunity. He knows there will be no marriage in heaven, so he is prepared to do without it already. Celibacy may have its difficulties, but such difficulties come when you live a dedicated, focused life.

A brief history of radical discipleship

While the steward's response to sexuality is very familiar to us, the radical's response seems, well, peculiar. But that has not always been so. The radical response traces its roots to Jesus and the requirements he made for his disciples while they were with him. It grew to dominate Christianity in the years after Constantine had turned the Roman empire to official Christianity. For a thousand years it was considered the normal way to best serve Jesus Christ.

When Constantine stopped the persecution of Christians, he changed the way Christians thought about spiritual life. For the first centuries, martyrdom and suffering had been dominant themes. Now they ended. Something far more dangerous than persecution invaded the church: the permissive, compromised attitudes of Rome. Seeking a deeper purity than they could find in their churches, some men and women went out into the desert. Anthony was one of these, a wealthy landowner who left all his possessions to pursue a life of prayer in the Egyptian desert. None of these early radicals had any idea of starting a movement, but they caught the imagination of other Christians dissatisfied with the lackadaisical status quo. More and more men and women followed them into the desert to pray.

Experience taught that not everyone could be an Anthony. He lived in complete solitude, but most people found the temptations of a life alone were too great. So monasteries were established— communes of people who lived simply, shared their few possessions, and kept certain standards of devotional life.

At the beginning, this was a simple and informal attempt to live a thoroughly committed life. But simplicity did not last. Over centuries monasteries grew large, sometimes wealthy and secure in their assertion of superior spirituality.

In the beginning, though, they must have shown an impressively genuine godliness. As the Roman empire became increasingly dissolute (under a Christian veneer) and was threatened by invasion, a life of Christian stewardship seemed more and more problematic. How could a person invest his life in the here and now when civilization showed signs of imminent destruction? The monks, because they had made a radical choice outside of the status quo, were able to live independently of the ups and downs of society. Everything was changing; they stayed the same.

Their radicalism was not pure, of course. An antimaterial, antisex, antifemale ideology seems to have infected the monks' way of thinking from the very beginning, which possibly explains why, rather than going out into the world and preaching the gospel as Jesus and Paul had, they removed themselves from society and went into the desert. (Later religious orders, however, such as the Franciscans and the Jesuits, were quite evangelistic.) The temptations of wealth and position and spiritual pride came, too. A monk might take a vow of poverty and then live in a palace. There was plenty of religious hypocrisy. Perhaps worst of all, monasticism developed a theory of salvation that seemed almost scientifically institutionalized. The grace of God no longer seemed necessary—or, more accurately, it was simply taken for granted. This was the "ladder of angels" that Luther rejected.

By no means would I call for a return to monasticism. Yet I would find it strange if a response to God that was so appealing to centuries of Christians had nothing worthwhile in it. Radicalism continually reasserts itself under different disguises, particularly when the church grows fat or the times are unusually threatened. Dietrich Bonhoeffer, in *The Cost of Discipleship* and *Life Together*, written during the years after Hitler came to power, promoted a form of radical discipleship. During the 1960s, some radicalism came back into American Protestantism. Christian communes were launched in which all members had to share alike and live a simple life, and in which obedience to the spiritual leaders of the group was considered an essential vow of membership. In some respects, too, the modern missionary movement is radical. Missionaries are usually expected (as pastors, for example, are not) to live simply and to obey their leaders in the mission society.

Strangely, though, the value of celibacy has not reasserted itself. We have a large population of singles who need to be celibate. Yet they feel this as a punishment. Is it possible they could see it, instead, as an opportunity?

A special calling?

There are objections to preaching positive celibacy. Some Christians say that celibacy is a special calling, given only to a few. It cannot be forced on someone. "Involuntary celibacy" is a contradiction in terms.

For example, Helmut Thielicke, writing to suggest tolerance of homosexual alliances, says that "Celibacy cannot be used as a counter-argument, because celibacy is based upon a special calling and, moreover, is an act of free will" (italics deleted).

It is difficult to see how this claim could be justified. The only passage in Scripture that might suggest that celibacy is a special, voluntary calling would be Jesus' words in Matthew 19, in which he says, in response to the disciples' shock over the indissolubility of marriage, "Not everyone can accept this word, but only those to whom it has been given. For some are eunuchs because they were born that way; others were made that way by men; and others have made themselves eunuchs because of the kingdom of heaven. The one who can accept this should accept it" (vv. 11–12).

This saying, commentators admit, is somewhat enigmatic. If Jesus were saying that celibacy must be a special calling, he would apparently identify "this word" (which only those to whom it has been given can accept) with celibacy. This is how Geoffrey Bromiley takes it: "A gift is needed if a person separated from a former spouse is to live without remarrying." The trouble with this interpretation is that Jesus has not mentioned a word about life without remarriage. He has spoken about the purity of marriage, which cannot be broken for any reason. "This word" would seem to be the demand for a pure monogamy. Who can live with the absolute demands of Christian marriage? Only those to whom it has been given. But Jesus immediately speaks of another possibility: that of celibacy, which some have because of their birth, some because of their experiences, and some because of their choice to live for the kingdom of God.

One would not want to stake too much on an interpretation of this difficult passage. But Paul's words in 1 Corinthians 7 seem crystal clear: Marriage and celibacy are equally a free choice. Paul gives no hint that marriage is normal and celibacy an unusual "special" condition for those who are called to it. He personally favors one choice (celibacy), but he recognizes that another might be best for others. He does speak of "gifts," but the implication is that either marriage or celibacy might be one's gift. "I wish that all men were as I am. But each man has his own gift from God; one has this gift, another has that" (1 Cor. 7:7).

Paul's judgment is that a person is best off staying in the situation in which he finds himself. These include conditions in which he clearly had no choice. "Was a man uncircumcised when he was called? He should not be circumcised. . . . Were you a slave when you were called? Don't let it trouble you—although if you can gain your freedom, do so. . . . Now about virgins . . . I think that it is good for you to remain as you are. Are you married? Do not seek a divorce. Are you unmarried? Do not look for a wife. But if you do marry, you have not sinned" (7:18–28).

The only "special calling" Paul recognizes is the calling to be the Lord's servant. A person can answer that call in any condition—circumcised or uncircumcised, slave or free, married or single. Single people may marry if they wish—but they are equally free to stay single. The only thing that matters is living obediently before God. He calls each one of us to be his own. That calling does not usually change our situation. It transforms it into a Christian vocation.

Not everyone who goes without sex is celibate in the sense that Paul would want him to be, for not everyone is entirely devoted to the Lord and answers Christ's calling as a single person. But that such a calling would be entirely good for any single person—indeed, the best of all options—Paul obviously did not doubt. He certainly did not think he was recommending it to one in a thousand "peculiar" Corinthians.

Living like a blind man

Paul's recommendation is hard for us to reconcile with what we feel about single life. How could he recommend a way of life that is, for most people, so miserable? Even those who recommend celibacy under certain circumstances acknowledge its misery. For example, John White in *Eros Defiled:* "What has life to offer you if marriage and normal sexual relations will never be yours? . . . Are we implying by our question that you are worse off than other people? If so we must stop right here. You *are* worse off—*in one way.* So is a blind man or a deaf man. . . . You have a personal tragedy. . . . If you want to spend the rest of your life feeling bitter and sorry for yourself, you will have only yourself to blame for your suffering."

A lot can be said for a stiff upper lip. We all certainly need one at times, and single people, oppressed by our society's glorification of marriage, need one often. But is life without sex necessarily a crippled existence? Is single life at best like a blind person making do in spite of his handicap? Very clearly, Paul could not have imagined so. He wrote of the privations he experienced—poverty, beatings, shipwrecks—but never included singleness. No doubt we are all affected by our experiences, and Paul's experiences included meeting the risen Jesus. Can anyone imagine comparing Jesus' life, single as it was, to that of a blind man or a deaf man? For that matter, should we pity a Saint Francis, a Mother Teresa, a C. S. Lewis (celibate for nearly all his life)? No doubt they had special abilities and unusual faith to live as they did. We cannot very well require that every single person live as admirably as they lived. But at least they raise our hopes. Perhaps being single is not always a handicap.

Some point out that single people—particularly single males—are prone to violence and suicide in our society. They are right: being single is often difficult—painfully so. But is the difficulty intrinsic to singleness, or is it rooted in the powerfully antisingle feelings of our society? If single people were in a supportive environment, would they have the same difficulty? Did monks, for instance, tend toward violence and suicide?

Others say that a single person's misery has a basis in Scripture. At the foundation of the universe, God said, "It is not good for the man to be alone" (Gen. 2:18). Adam needed a helpmate, and God's company was no substitute.

Adam, however, was not the Bible's last word on sexuality. The New Testament introduces something new. Jesus will take us not simply to Eden, but beyond Eden. He himself is the best evidence of where we are going. "It is not good for man to be alone." Was Jesus' life then "not good"?

Of course it was very good. And he is not, and has never been, alone. From the beginning he was in fellowship with the Father (as Adam, and we, cannot be). He calls us to a fellowship like that with each other. Jesus prayed just before his death, "I pray also for those who will believe in me through their message, that all of them may be one, Father, just as you are in me and I am in you. . . . I have given them the glory that you gave me, that they may be one as we are one. . . . May they be brought to complete unity to let the world know that you sent me and have loved them even as you have loved me" (John 17:20–23). Anyone experiencing such oneness with other believers is not really alone any longer.

Going without sex is not, per se, gracious or beautiful. A person who cannot marry and yet cannot accept his situation will feel the "not good" of being alone. Life in the kingdom, however, ought to transform his situation. He is no longer alone, for he has become a member of a family. Making this real for single people should be as important for the church as its concern for strong marriages. Whether celibacy is for life, or for a short period, the need is the same.

Paul's mention of slavery (1 Cor. 7:21–23) puts all this in an interesting, and realistic, light. Paul makes it clear that no one wants to be a slave. "If you can gain your freedom, do so." We may feel the same about our sexual condition, married or single. Just as the slave ached for freedom, so a single person may ache for sexual intimacy, and a married person may ache to be released from a partner. But the coming of Jesus transforms ordinary judgments. "He who was a slave when he was called by the Lord is the Lord's freedman; similarly, he who was a free man when he was called is Christ's slave. You were bought at a price; do not become slaves of men." In marriage or in singleness, we can serve Christ. That is genuine freedom.

Mike was 32 and unmarried. That was not the problem he presented to his pastor when he came in for counseling; he rambled on and on about his inability to make lasting friendships, his loneliness, his feeling that people in the church were superficially friendly but really had no time for him. But as the talk went on, George, his pastor, thought increasing-

ly that Mike's real problem was the lack of a wife.

Mike was probably 30 pounds overweight, short, and balding; he had a solid but ordinary job as a lab technician. He would make a good husband, George thought—a steady provider. But it would take just the right woman to see him as a catch. He was so bland. And he was so desperate.

George tried to help Mike think through some ways that he could meet women in an unthreatening, hopeful situation. He recommended a singles group at the Baptist church. (He apologized that they had never managed to get something like it going in their church. "That's one of my dreams," he told Mike.) Then he prayed for Mike, asking God to bring the right girl along at the right time. "We trust you for this, Lord, in the name of Jesus."

After Mike left, George felt discouraged. He knew he had hit the nail on the head, zeroing in on singleness. The problem was how to change it. Sometimes, when you saw somebody like Mike, you wished we could go back to arranged marriages. Then no one would be left out.

Sexual salvation works both ways. Not only does salvation in Christ transform our sexuality, but our sexuality becomes a sign of the kingdom. The way we live as sexual creatures ought to witness that Jesus is Lord.

How can celibacy witness to anything besides misanthropy? Let Irene Kassorla once again speak for pop psychology: "James Thurber once asked the question, 'Is sex necessary?' My immediate answer is an unqualified *yes.* . . . While one could certainly argue that it is possible to survive without sex . . . or walks in the park, or music, or laughter, or the other sweet extras of living that are *not* primary biological needs. . . .

"WHY SHOULD YOU?"

Kassorla explains that when you try to repress your erotic sensuality, you inevitably repress all your emotions. She considers an active sex life to be an essential ingredient for a stable personality. "Too many women I've treated," she says, "repress their normal sexual functioning. . . . Often a closer examination of their emotional profiles reveals that these sexually sterile women have rigid and peculiar personalities, as well."

Note that this is not worlds away from John White's comparison of celibacy to blindness or deafness. One may claim that the handicapped can make the best of life within their limitations. But who would choose to be blind? And how can a disability be, in any way, a sign of the kingdom?

The joys of self-control?
One answer has been given repeatedly over the centuries: A celibate person demonstrates self-control. By doing without something as attractive as sex, he demonstrates that his mind and spirit have gained control over the body's appetites. Gandhi, for instance, gave up sleeping with his wife, but he would take a beautiful young woman to bed with him in order to develop his own self-mastery.

In Jesus and his disciples, and in Paul, there was no hint of such an asceticism. They were not celibate to prove their own mastery. They were celibate because their singleness enabled them to serve God in a way that would otherwise have been impossible. They lived with a singleness of purpose, a "single eye." In Paul's words, they showed "an undivided devotion to the Lord" (1 Cor. 7:35).

Married people, after all, need self-control too, sometimes in situations that are just as difficult as those single people face. People in marriages get violently angry, for instance, and yet they have to live together.

What celibacy does show, in a way that marriage cannot, is a singleness of purpose. This is what all radical Christianity tries to demonstrate: that everyday demands of living should not get in the way of spontaneous, unreserved obedience to Christ's command to love God and our neighbor. Someone who gives away his property does so not to demonstrate asceticism, but to remove the barrier that caring for property makes to his freedom to serve God. Someone who chooses nonviolence does so because self-defense often compromises his ability to love his neighbor. Similarly, celibacy removes the barriers marriage puts up to spontaneous love of God and neighbor. A good spouse must give some priority to his family; he cannot easily be radical when he has children.

Consider Jesus. It is impossible to imagine a more singleminded person. Throughout his ministry he knew his business exactly. He could not be dissuaded from his agenda by the concerns of the crowds, the criticisms of the Pharisees, or the fears and hopes of his disciples. He "resolutely set his face to go to Jerusalem" (Luke 9:51) to his own death. This picture of Jesus steadfastly choosing to give his life is the greatest sign of the kingdom; everywhere the kingdom has been preached the cross has been used as a shorthand symbol for that single-minded self-sacrifice.

But could Jesus have made these choices if he were married and had a family to care for? Perhaps; but certainly not so freely. Neither could Paul have dedicated his life in the same degree to planting churches if he had needed to share his concern with a wife and family.

A single person is not necessarily a sign of the kingdom. If he is tangled in his longings and his sense of loss, he is not. But a single person can demonstrate with a remarkable clarity that he knows the reason he was created: to love and serve God, and him only. If that singleness of vision, that purity of heart, possesses him and shows itself in his purposeful service of others and in his preoccupation with prayer and worship, then he makes a radical statement with his life about the kingdom.

Mother Teresa does this in our century. She is an implacable reminder that there is another kingdom. She cares for the dying, who have no value in this world, because she believes they have value in the next. It is very difficult to imagine any married person calling the world to account in quite her way.

Not many will match Mother Teresa. But in smaller and quieter ways, every single person can make the same witness. He or she can step beyond his or her own wishes and drives, to be devoted to a more driving concern. Such a purpose can transform a single person's sexual satisfaction, but more important, it can point beyond sexuality to the cross. This will probably always be "foolishness to the Gentiles." What, after all, is a Mother Teresa when stacked up against the power of Wall Street? Or Hollywood? But for those with the ears to hear and the eyes to see, a Mother Teresa (and her many single brothers and sisters) will evoke an invisible power before which they too must bow.

This is what George, the pastor, can offer Mike. It is all very well to plot strategies for meeting marriageable women, but what does that have to do with the kingdom of God? If the strategies fail, is Mike's life then condemned to failure? Of course not. It cannot be easy, in our society, to enable Mike to shift his gaze from the promise of sex and intimacy to the promise of a radical dedication to God's kingdom. Even if he is willing to move in that direction, he will almost certainly feel depressed and lonely at times over what he feels he has lost. Married people feel depressed and lonely often enough too, of course, but perhaps less than Mike will, for they have the affirmation and support of our society.

If George feels hesitant to speak to Mike about such a difficult, radical path, he ought to go back to the New Testament and read again what Jesus promised to his disciples. They, too, were called to be witnesses of an invisible kingdom. They, too, were asked to give up family and friends, at least for a time. They were not called as disciples with promises of warmth and intimacy, however much they may (or may not) have experienced warmth and intimacy along the way. They were called to be servants of Jesus. They answered. They did not regret it.

Marriage as a sign

I have already attempted to explore how marriage may, in two ways, be a sign of the kingdom. An "easy" marriage shows the love for another that is spontaneous, joyful, and naturally unselfish. Love is somehow drawn out of us, without effort. Such love points beyond our world to a better world where love reigns.

In a "hard" marriage—and all marriages are hard at least some of the time—we discover love that endures in a sinful world, love that is passionate and simply will not let go of the beloved. Such love sometimes makes no sense in practical terms. Yet love that perseveres through pain points to something beyond our world, to a God who clings to his people passionately, despite their unfaithfulness.

Perhaps it is valuable to note that in the Bible, sex itself is not referred to as a sign. Marriage is a sign; sex is not. This stands out when you compare Christianity to other religions, such as Hinduism, in which sex is sacramental, and the erotic interplay of two persons is connected closely to the relationship between God and humanity. Stories of the Hindu gods often have plainly erotic meanings, perhaps most notably in the case of Krishna and the cowgirls: As a prank he stole their clothes as they bathed in the river, and made them come to him naked, with their hands on their heads. "This story of full frontal nudity," writes Geoffrey Parrinder, "still popular in verse and painting, was given mystical interpretations of the nakedness of the soul before God." Krishna and one of the girls, Radha, became lovers, "her sexual passion and adultery in leaving her husband indicating the priority which God required in loving devotion."

In the sacred Upanishads, intercourse is described as a religious ceremony: "Her lap is a sacrificial altar, her pubic hairs are the sacrificial grass. . . ." When a man wanted to conceive a son, he sprinkled the woman with water three times, saying, "I am this man, you are that woman . . . I am heaven, you are earth." He opened her thighs saying, "Spread yourselves apart, heaven and earth."

According to Parrinder, not only was sexual intercourse understood in religious terms, but religious rituals were given detailed sexual interpretations. For example, "if in the course of a recitation the priest separated the first two quarters of a verse and brought the other two close together, this was said to be happening because a woman separates her thighs during copulation and the man presses them together."

I raise this to bring out the distinctiveness of Christianity. Its focus is not on any sacramental meaning of sex, but on the meaning of marriage. In the Bible, the lasting and loving bond between two people signifies God's kingdom; sex has great meaning to the partners within that bond, but in itself it reveals nothing about God.

In Christian thinking, sex serves marriage—it is not that marriage serves sex. Marriage is not merely a license for sex, or a way of regulating passion. Marriage takes priority. Why so? Sex seems so real, so physical, while marriage can disappear at the whim of either partner.

I suspect it is so because marriage is, as sex is not, an act of faith—in fact, a life of faith. We know why people have sex. They do so because they desire each other, and count on pleasure. Why do people marry, however? Why do they promise to love and serve each other forever? No calculation of their interests can justify it. Absolute commitment tends to lead to happiness, as we have seen, but an absolute commitment cannot be based on the expectation of happiness—since happiness cannot be guaranteed.

Marriage is an act of faith, and a life of faith. This faith is a response to the person you love. Because of who your lover is, and your lover's irreplaceable value to you, you promise to love and cherish until death. Whether your marriage is easy or hard, you start over on this journey of faith every day.

Where marriages are pure and loving, where they endure through the years and through all kinds of troubles, where both man and woman sacrifice for each other, not because they count on a reward of happiness but because they see each other as persons of infinite value—where such marriages are known, people will see beyond the scrawny calculations that move our world. They will see another world, ruled by a sacrificial lamb.

Which way is best?

There are two kinds of signs in our sexuality. These signs are very different from each other, and in our history one has tended to dominate the other. For centuries, celibacy was considered the main entrance to sexual salvation, with marriage a kind of back door for the rabble. Then, after the Reformation, marriage took over the front door, and single people were sent to the back. They became peculiar, crippled people; their best hope was to overcome their handicap.

Can the two signs coexist? Can we value them both? The early church did. Most of the apostles did their work in tandem with a believing wife; Paul, Barnabas, and Timothy apparently did theirs alone (1 Cor. 9:5). Paul recommended celibacy to the Corinthians, but to the Ephesians he compared marriage to the love of Christ for the church. Jesus was celibate, yet he attended a wedding and blessed its celebration with a miracle. When Paul wrote to Timothy, he sanctioned a group of older women who had evidently taken a celibate vow, dedicating their lives to Christ's ministry; but he recommended that younger women not take such a vow, since they tended to change their minds and wish to marry (1 Tim. 5:9–15). In a very practical way, he honored the possibilities and difficulties of both ways of life.

Nowhere in Scripture is there any sign of preferring one form of sexual witness over another, except in Paul's carefully hedged recommendation of celibacy to the Corinthians. Historians say that the early centuries of the church show the same pattern: single people and married people together, valuing each other's gifts.

Today no one can doubt that we need all the witness to Christ we can muster, and that sexuality is an area where our witness is most vulnerable and under attack. Can we afford to let any of our gifts go unrecognized?

Chapter 9

FOUR WAYS BACK TO EDEN

I would like to return to considering the sexual revolution. Some say the sexual revolution has already failed, that the pendulum is swinging back to the Old Consensus. I see few signs of this. If the sexual revolution represents the latest manifestation of a cultural tide more than two centuries old, it is not likely to stop in a decade. Many aspects of the sexual revolution seem irreversible:

- Serial marriage, in which divorce and remarriage are widely accepted;
- The end of the double standard between men and women for sexual conduct;
- Open discussion of sex between men and women and in public media;
- The common use of erotic visual images in advertising, television, and numerous other media;
- A large amount of medical knowledge about the body's sexuality;
- The possibility of separating sex from procreation;
- A pervasive popular Freudianism, in which all activity is thought to have its roots in sexual impulses;

- A strong faith that sex is one of life's most important sources of happiness and meaning.

Other features seem less certain to last, but nonetheless show few signs of disappearing:

- Tolerance for certain deviations from the norm, such as adultery or homosexuality;
- The devaluation of virginity;
- A positive value for premarital sexual experimentation, for both men and women.

Many features of the sexual revolution are horrific to thoughtful Christians. We feel dismay regarding its lack of ethical standards and the harm to innocent people it often carelessly sanctions. I am thinking particularly of the injury sustained by millions of teenage girls and by millions of middle-aged divorced women. Of course, their causes are taken up by some leaders of the sexual revolution— but never as though the sexual revolution itself bore any responsibility for their pain.

On the other hand, it seems obvious that Christians owe some thanks to the sexual revolution. I would list three positive qualities. One is the sexual revolution's affirmation of creation. The sexual revolution has repeatedly told us that sex is good and that bodies are good, and the idea has taken hold. Several evangelical Christian sex manuals have become best-selling books in the past decade. Surely they were more immediately inspired by Masters and Johnson than by the Bible.

A second positive quality is the end of the double standard. For perhaps the first time in history, women are judged by the same moral standard as men. This is a triumph of justice.

A third positive quality of the sexual revolution is its recognition that something is wrong with the way we live our sexuality. According to some, the problem is repression; according to others, it is sex-role stereotypes. Regardless of what explanations are given, few claim that sexuality is purely good in the way we experience it. Rather, it ought to be good but something has gone wrong. With this general proposition, Christians will agree.

Early in this book I offered a broad critique of the sexual revolution. In one sense, a Christian's view of the sexual revolution is of a road that forks in two directions. In one direction is a Christian view of sexual salvation; in the other direction is the false salvation offered by the sexual revolution. The choice is either/or.

Since the sexual revolution is not going away, however, and since we will have to live with it in this world, we also need a subtler understanding of it. In this chapter I want briefly to examine four pathways out of our problems that are frequently proposed by modern secularists. These pathways do not deal so much with sexual salvation itself as with what might be called the means of salvation. The four pathways are equality, education, freedom, and privacy. We will see that Christians share an appreciation for these pathways—and have some distinctive perspectives to share.

Equality between male and female

What is wrong with sex as we know it? One answer given is sexism. According to this analysis, rigid gender roles have inhibited both men and women from finding their true selves, virtually destroying their potential for sexual enjoyment. Women were told not to enjoy sex, but to endure it. Men lost touch with their feelings, due to the pressure to perform. Shirley Luthman writes, "I am convinced that we have no realistic knowledge about what males are capable of sexually because most males in our culture express their sexuality according to a program of performance. I think that if they learned to experience sex as part of their self-expression and as a result of a flow between the male and female, our whole concept of male sexuality would change."

For a time this appeared to have happened, as book after book celebrated woman's endless erotic potential, while providing detailed instructions on the man's responsibility to let down his emotional defenses and join this pleasure. In the movies, all the women were equal partners in sexual desire, and all the good men knew how to cry. It appeared as though a huge increase in erotic pleasure had entered American bedrooms, and that men and women were happily experimenting with not merely new positions, but new, interchangeable roles.

By now, much of that early euphoria has disappeared. But that should not obscure the fact that something monumental has occurred. Until recently, in every time and every place we know of, men have dominated and used women as though they were less than human. It was so wherever and whenever you looked, from classical Greece to traditional Africa.

Sociobiologists and anthropologists usually relate gender roles to the necessities of raising children: for example, they note that nursing babies restricted the movements of primitive women, who relied on males to hunt for food and protect them from enemies until their child was weaned. Anthropologists work out complicated hypotheses about how social systems evolved from this.

Whatever the truth of such hypotheses, no one can doubt that gender roles became more than convenient divisions of labor. An ideology accompanied them, an ideology of male superiority and control. An aphorism from ancient Greece, attributed to Demosthenes, expresses it like a mathematical equation: "Mistresses we keep for the sake of pleasure, concubines for the daily care of our persons, but wives to bear us legitimate children and to be faithful guardians of our households." Obviously, these were not reciprocal relationships. The man and his needs were at the center of a network of women. The double standard was absolute, as it was in virtually every civilization before our era. In no civilization were women thought to be equal to men in their intrinsic worth. That idea would have been alien to Plato and Aristotle, Buddha and Confucius.

The monotonous pattern of male control has now been broken, at least in principle, in the West. Under the law women are treated virtually the same as men. Women can and do form lives independent of men; they even raise children virtually without the aid of men. Women are educated in the same manner as men, and they hold the same kinds of jobs. The double standard of sexual morality has been practically eliminated; what men can do, women can do, too.

Still, many of the old ways continue. Women earn less than men. They are far more likely to be poor. Married women cannot count on their husbands' help with domestic chores—dishes, diapers, laundry—no matter how many hours the women work outside the home. Women still suffer from rape and domestic violence. In many ways, women's liberation is far from done. But from the perspective of history, we have already seen earth-shaking changes.

Inner liberation

From the first, liberation has been understood to affect inner values as well as outward circumstances. It would never be enough to change the laws. The ideology of male dominance had to be changed. Women had to stop living just to please men, and men had to learn to respect women's ambitions. This was just as true in the bedroom as anywhere else.

The problem, of course, has been what to replace the old gender roles with. If men and women are not to be masculine and feminine, as traditionally understood, what should they be? Theorists become vague on this point. They prefer, naturally, to wax eloquent on the wonderful benefits that will come when we get rid of the last vestiges of the old, narrow stereotypes.

One tendency has been to rely on a word that has served well in legal contexts: *equality*. Women and men are recognized as equals under the law: Their votes are equal, their standing in court is equal. They should receive equal opportunities and equal pay. But the word has been applied beyond the legal context; it tends to be broadened, to mean "identical." For, in a society that rewards each person according to his or her ability, how can two people be of equal worth unless they have equal ability? And as that equality is applied to more and more specific contexts—to physical education, to jobs as diverse as nursing and heavy-equipment operation—there is a tendency to slip into thinking of men and women as undifferentiated in nature, rather than merely under law.

How do men and women become identical? A human being had to be invented: the androgynous person. An androgynous person is one who recognizes both "masculine" and "feminine" traits within himself, and believes that his sex is irrelevant for discovering his true nature. For such a person, there are no definite patterns of relationships between the sexes; each person, each encounter, is unique. According to James Nelson, "If we accept the fact that essentially we are androgynous, that each of us has a variety of capabilities and psychological tendencies that fall into both of the categories which society calls masculine and feminine, then to ask, 'Which of these is predominant in me?' is to ask the wrong question. We might better ask ourselves, 'What capacities within me, what gifts that I have been given, are called for in this particular situation?' " The freedom implicit in this is appealing, of course, but the underlying point is that "essentially we are androgynous," that is, there is no point in discussing men and women as such, since at the core they are the same.

For a time, the androgynous person fit with assertions—popular among social scientists—that the differences between men and women were unimportant. One noted sex researcher, John Money, indicated, "Sex differences are relative, not absolute. They can be assigned however we wish, as long as we allow for two simple facts: first, that men impregnate, women menstruate, gestate and lactate; and second, that adult individuals cannot alter the nuclear core of their gender schemes."

As time has passed, those two "simple facts" have seemed to grow less simple, and the sentence has begun to sound something like one reading, "The differences between humans and chimpanzees are relative, not absolute. They can be interchanged at will as long as we allow for two simple facts: chimps live in trees, and humans carry on conversation." After all, reproduction and child-rearing are fundamental preoccupations of most humans and of all cultures, and the unchangeable "nuclear core of our gender schemes" touches everything we do. "Baby hunger" is just one way in which those simple facts have loomed larger. Women who ignored their potential to raise children, emphasizing other possibilities, have found their bodies making an insistent claim on their attention.

Do our bodies make a difference?
Lisa Sowle Cahill puts the broader issue theologically: "Arguments that the sexes must in principle be identical in all characteristics and capacities seem to presuppose that sexual differentiation is merely accidental in relation to some human essence abstracted from the physical forms in which it invariably must be realized. Refusal to come to terms with the boundaries and possibilities that frame and make possible human choices is precisely the sin that propels the disaster of Genesis 3." In other words, we are not ethereal spirits with sexual organs stuck on as an afterthought; the differences in our bodies make a difference.

The "androgynous human" who explored his/her position along a masculine-feminine spectrum without much reference to his or her own gender—this theoretical person has lived a short theoretical life, it now seems. An awareness that male and female are constitutionally different has increasingly pervaded both secular and religious writings on sexuality. Carol Gilligan of Harvard has been particularly noted for attempting to describe these differences.

Where does this leave the possibility of overthrowing rigid gender distinctions? Sometimes it now seems that people are playing a game, hemmed in between their commitment to equality and their experience of differences. Take, for instance, this word from Alexandra Penney, in a *Ladies Home Journal* article entitled "Six Sex Mistakes Most Wives Make."

"[Men] want a woman to be the aggressor—sometimes—because the surprise of her taking the upper hand can provide a particularly delicious sexual frisson. However, a man wants a woman to do this only when he is comfortable with it. He still wants to feel that he is in the lead.

". . . No one says it is easy to make the switch from equal partner to surrendering mate—even though it can involve exquisite pleasure. . . . But the reality is this: If you want your relationship to make it, giving your man what he needs is what counts. And if that means letting him feel that he's in control during your most private moments, well. . . . As one woman told me recently, 'What's so terrible about giving in?' "

Granted that such words are hardly sanctioned by feminists, but they represent an increased "realism" employed by both men and women. Sometimes intimacy and equality seem to be in competition. For the sake of compromise, some may play a role, even though it involves hiding part of themselves. The utopia promised by freedom from restrictive gender differences seems far away.

Who kicked men off the throne?

If the history of the world is a monotonous story of male domination, why have men lost, or surrendered, control? One possible answer is that technology has made it inevitable. Work now requires much less brute strength, and very little mobility; women have fewer children and give less of their total life span to raising them. So the biological imperatives are no longer there.

To some extent, however, this answer begs the question. Why would men allow the technology to be used by women? Why relinquish the power as well as the technology, like foot binding and female circumcision, that reinforced the power? The answer, I believe, is that Christian morality undermined male domination.

According to philosopher Diogenes Allen, "Christianity is the source of the conviction that every person has an absolute value; it is not present in any philosophy prior to the advent of Christianity." It is quite true that Christianity did not have a social program to implement that value; slavery and the subordination of women went unopposed in Christendom for many centuries. However, the absolute value of persons, if not a rule on Earth, was certainly a rule in heaven. As Paul put it, "There is neither Jew nor Greek, there is neither slave nor free, there is neither male nor female; for you are all one in Christ Jesus" (Gal. 3:28). Even if nowhere else, women had absolute and equal value before God. That made a rather large crack in the ideology of male control.

Ultimately, the equal worth of women in God's eyes led to practical changes, most notably in education. Remember that almost all education in the West after the fall of Rome was promoted by the church, and for church purposes. Yet, from a very early date in Europe, "clerical" skills were useful in the affairs of state and commerce, and "clerics" (clerks) became the bureaucrats of society. When women gained access to Christian education, usually through the church and for the church's reasons, it was a huge step toward their economic and political equality.

Perhaps as subversive was another idea that Christianity introduced: mutual monogamy. Geoffrey Parrinder writes that "Christianity is the only major religion which from the outset has seemed to insist upon monogamy. . . . In theory monogamy should have offered the best opportunity for equal rights to husband and wife, and the highest regard for married love, but unhappily for many centuries such ideals were not the most cherished. . . ." On the other hand, they were never abandoned. The ideal of mutual fidelity was often ignored, but it remained the stated ideal. Like the absolute value of persons, mutual fidelity had subversive power. At about the time of the Reformation it began to be taken seriously. If husband and wife are equally responsible to each other for sexual fidelity, if neither is allowed any sexual alternative to play off against his spouse, then in principle they have equal sexual rights. Equal sexual fidelity has far more liberating potential than the kind of sexual equality we have actually gained, in which women can be as promiscuous as men.

So while it is true that many Christians have been (and still are) painstakingly slow to make way for female equality, it is equally true that Christianity broke the power of male domination, both in theory ("all are one in Christ") and ultimately in practice (in marriage and education).

Value in God's eyes

But where next? Is sexual equality bogged down, or will it further advance? Two distinctively Christian ideas can help clarify the discussion.

First, in the Christian's eyes equal worth is based on God's equal regard. When he cares for someone that person has value. Not all that he cares for equally must be identical. On the contrary, it is their splendid variety that he loves.

Thus equality is based not on findings that women score as well on IQ tests as do men, or that they have an equally stable emotional makeup, any more than it would depend in an agrarian society on women demonstrating equal physical strength. Men and women may be as different as anyone can imagine, and still be equal—equally deserving of respect, of justice, of status. Equality based on identity must always be subject to the latest proof. Equality based on God's revelation about what matters to him cannot be shaken.

Second, the pervasive personalism of the Bible, the concern for real people, and not for abstract principles about people—such as masculinity and femininity—keeps us from too rigid a set of prescriptions for male and female roles. There is a strong tendency to discuss this subject as though people had to fit an abstraction. On one side, a man should "act like a man," or on the other side, men and women should prefer the same careers and the same programs in school, and if they don't it is proof of discrimination. Men and women are not called to live up to ideals of masculine and feminine; it is not some abstract "balance" between the male and female principles (as in Confucian "Yin-Yang" philosophy) that matters. Men and women are called into community as the persons that they are, with all their individual variation, and their body-and-soul differences between men and women.

This is not at all to say that they can just "be themselves," living free from all gender roles. On the contrary, men and women have specific role responsibilities, depending on the covenants they are in with regard to each other—husband and wife, father and son, father and daughter, mother and son, mother and daughter, sister and sister, brother and brother, brother and sister. These are covenants with men and women, boys and girls—not androgynous persons. Loving will always see this realistically. It will not pretend that "the guys" will have the same way of interacting as "the girls." But loving will see the person of a particular gender, not a person who must live up (or down) to his or her particular gender. It will not insist that a woman meet certain abstract feminine characteristics. No one, in Christian light, should need to play at being what he or she is not.

A third point may be added: Christians should always oppose the degradation of women, though without any naïveté that it will be utterly eradicated by a social program. The power struggles between men and women appear as part of God's curse on humankind, pronounced to Eve in Genesis 3:16—"Your desire shall be for your husband, and he shall rule over you." We can expect the curse to continue wherever the curse of sin holds sway.

Yet the curse ought never to be turned into the norm. It ought to be seen for what it is—a bitter fruit of our alienation from God and one another. In this viewpoint there is hope. To the extent that our alienation from God is healed, we can expect to see the end of male domination.

The young dentist and his wife of three years were deeply in love, but his wife had never reached orgasm during their marriage. He found this almost as frustrating as she did. . . . Their sexual frustration soon produced marital conflict. . . .

One Sunday morning their pastor was preaching on the text, "In all thy ways acknowledge Him, and He shall direct thy paths." They heard him say, "You do not have a problem in your life that you cannot take to the Lord in prayer." The dentist looked at his wife and realized that they had not prayed about it. Afterward they discussed it and decided to do so.

On Friday of that week they were invited to a social gathering. Being the first to arrive, they were ushered into the family room to await the arrival of the other guests. It was a large room with a couple of conversation areas, so they chose a couch on the far side of the room. They were no sooner seated than another couple came in and sat on the first couch behind them, a large floral arrangement preventing the dentist and his wife from being seen by the new arrivals. Thinking they were alone, this sanguine husband put his arm around his wife and exclaimed, "Hasn't our relationship been beautiful since we discovered clitoral stimulation?" The dentist silently glanced at his wife and thought, "We have never tried that." That night they did, and it was the beginning of a new experience for them both.

With obvious emotion the dentist told me, "That simple technique was like a key that opened the door to a beautiful relationship which we have enjoyed for the past three years."
—Tim and Beverly LaHaye, *The Act of Marriage*

The second pathway to sexual salvation I want to consider is education. It is usually associated with optimistic secular humanists, who might say, "Nine-tenths of the world's problems are caused by ignorance and superstition."

Yet a conservative Christian like Tim LaHaye, who believes that at least nine-tenths of the world's problems are caused by sin, believes in sex education. In this story, he regards it as an answer to prayer. He writes, "The average woman knows far more about the operation of her sewing machine than she does her own reproductive organs." The resulting ignorance he lists as number one among the factors keeping women from orgasmic pleasure.

America has long been a nation committed to education as a kind of redeemer, and with sex it is no different. Dr. Ruth remembers sadly the days when "nowhere was there any sensible, reliable information on the air about real-life sex, in an era when unwanted pregnancies and venereal disease and broken homes were all stemming from ignorance about this central fact of life!" She is optimistic: "We have seen a virtual explosion of new scientific information about sex, as well as significant advances in the diagnosis and treatment of sexual disorders. We are now at a point where we understand sexual development[!] and know what it takes to prevent and treat many of the sexual problems that just a few years ago were believed to be beyond control."

I suspect that Tim LaHaye is unenthusiastic about Dr. Ruth's idea of education, and even less enthusiastic about Planned Parenthood's. In fact, one of the battlegrounds of the sexual revolution has become sex education in the schools. Why? One objection of conservative Christians is that the education provided in public schools is "thin." It is usually mere biology. When more than biology is offered, sex is discussed in a "value-free" context. Conservatives say: Surely the material would be better discussed in a family setting, where parental love and example would place sexuality in its proper context.

But Planned Parenthood does not argue against the proposition that parents *ought* to be providing sex education. They simply point out that parents don't. Sex education is so critical, advocates say, that it simply cannot be left to the whims of parents. The state must provide it. The state is incompetent to teach "values"; that may be left to parents and churches. But it is urgent that biological facts be known.

Preventing pregnancies

Why do they think biology is so urgently necessary for children? The main reason, obviously, is birth control. The number of out-of-wedlock teenage pregnancies is alarming to all. A Louis Harris survey done for Planned Parenthood in 1986 showed that sexually active teenagers who had had comprehensive sex education, either from their parents or in school, were considerably more likely to use birth control methods. Dismayingly, though, less than half the sexually active teenagers who had the highest knowledge of sex and birth control said they used birth control methods all the time. Slightly over half had used birth control the first time they had sex. "Unexpected sex," not ignorance, was the most common reason for not using birth control.

"This whole notion of sex as something that most people are 'swept away' by is a major problem, potentially attributable to the media which overly romanticizes sex," said Faye Wattleton, president of Planned Parenthood. "It leads teenagers to believe that people never expect to have sex—that planning to have sex is a bad thing. This idea is not only preposterous, it is extremely dangerous. And until we create a social climate in which sex is spoken about in clear and open terms and people are able to acknowledge that they are going to have sex, we will continue to see the disastrous consequences that we are seeing today."

Thus Planned Parenthood's educational solution requires more than mere information. Knowledge helps, but in the current environment it would not come close to eliminating our troubles. That requires a social climate that is deromanticized and realistic. Teenagers must learn to talk openly about sex, to acknowledge their own plans as freely as they acknowledge their plans to, say, attend a concert. How this revolution in consciousness will come, Planned Parenthood does not seem so clear about. The idea would appear to be that the more we talk about sex, the less romanticized it will seem. So far, the evidence in support of this proposition is lacking. Never has sex been so talked about. Yet sex seems at least as romanticized as it was during the Victorian period—if by romanticism we mean the idea that sex is "bigger than both of us," that it can sweep people away, that it has transcendent significance.

Information is unable to solve most adult sexual problems, either. Andrew Greeley expresses this limitation in typically pungent language. "The currently popular sex books . . . shed rather little light on complexities and confusions of human behavior. It is, after all, of only small moment to know how fellatio is performed and to be told that there is 'nothing wrong' with it when one is always fighting with the wife and finding it difficult to keep hands off the women in the office and feeling plenty guilty about both. Nor do the details of female orgasm help much when one is trying to work up enough nerve to attempt a reconciliation in a love grown sour."

One could make the same kind of comments regarding teenage sex. It is of little help to know what condoms are, and where to get them, if you lack the respect for your life and others' lives to treat your sexuality as something to be used reverently.

Wisdom and sex education

The biblical concept of wisdom is an important corrective to the idea of salvation through education. In Judeo-Christian thinking, education is highly honored. The Jews have always been "people of the Book," and that presupposes education. But it could never be "value-free" education. Mere facts must be related to people. They must also be related to God. And no deed can be discussed without considering its contribution to a whole way of life.

What does this say about Planned Parenthood's desire to "create a social climate in which sex is spoken about in clear and open terms and people are able to acknowledge that they are going to have sex"? It means that merely candid talk is very far from adequate. The question is: *What will be said in those clear and open terms?* When people acknowledge their plans, what will those plans be, and how will they contribute to their development into mature, righteous human beings?

Wisdom, as it is presented in the Book of Proverbs, treats living as a skill. Proverbs teaches everything from the etiquette of greeting people too cheerfully in the morning, to the way in which money and friendship interact. It is parent-to-child counsel, covering a huge variety of topics. Factual information is integrated with morality. Proverbs does not merely pass on information; it attempts to train a person's character.

Christians certainly ought to be against ignorance, and for scientific understanding of sexuality. We can welcome the research done by Masters and Johnson and their heirs, and utilize their specialized knowledge to relieve misery. Who can fail to rejoice, along with Tim LaHaye, when a struggling couple achieves sexual satisfaction through an understanding of sexual technique? Yet Christians will always press for a wider understanding of sexuality, one that embraces all of life. At this point in time, our society offers no way to pass on sexual wisdom to the next generation. It will not happen in health classes, and wisdom about sex is certainly not being transmitted by television sets. Unfortunately, it is not being transmitted in church, either, or in many of the living rooms of families that attend church.

One Sunday night at WYNY I took a call that went like this. I opened one of the waiting lines and said, "Hello, you're on the air."

"Uh, hi," a man said. "My girl friend and I just broke up over something stupid. If she eats a crunchy peanut butter sandwich, she gets very horny. But there are certain things I don't think are right. If I go to bed with someone, I don't want to go to bed with her and peanut butter."

"Look, I understand," I said. "If both people would like to go to bed with peanut butter, I would say that if you use contraceptives, that's all right. The moment only one person likes peanut butter and the other doesn't, then you have to take a stand."

In the infinite varieties of sex there are things you will want to do and things you won't. . . . There are things you want to do very much, things you will do to please the other person, and things that—yech! Don't be pressured into doing things you really don't want to do. . . . In fact, don't be pressured into having sex at all if you don't want to—not to be in with your crowd, not to show someone that you really do love him or her. You have a right to your boundaries. Stick up for them.

What you might not want to do may only involve peanut butter, but if you feel strongly about it, stick up for your individual rights.

If it happens that you do want peanut butter in bed while you're

having sex and your partner doesn't, in the long run the thing to do may be to find another partner. There are millions of people out there who won't mind peanut butter at all, may like it a lot, or may even get to like it as much as you do.
                    —Dr. Ruth Westheimer, *Dr. Ruth's Guide to Good Sex*

What does Dr. Ruth believe in? Certainly she believes in the first two aspects I have discussed: equality for men and women, and education. At least as much, though, she believes in freedom. That is the third pathway to sexual salvation I want to consider.

Dr. Ruth's idea of freedom is not the freedom of libertines—only the freedom to do. She encourages people *not* to do, if they choose. For example, she expresses support for religious scruples:

"An Orthodox Jew, or a devout Catholic, or a strict Baptist, or anybody like that has my respect.

"I don't believe that the first thing for them to do is to get rid of religious restrictions."

Yet the foundation of freedom is, for her—peanut butter. If you feel strongly about wanting to do something, you do it. If you don't want to do something, you don't. And if you can't reach an agreeable compromise with your partner, look for another partner. Peanut butter, anal sex, devout Catholicism, they are all on the same plane. It only matters that each person knows what he or she likes, and pursues it. That's freedom: unstructured space. The individual makes his or her own structure.

The noble sexual savage
Behind this kind of freedom is Rousseau's great myth of the noble savage—the human being who is naturally good and happy so long as he is left to his own blessed instincts. He will certainly not destroy himself by doing what he likes! America's latest fling with Rousseau began in the sixties, when "free love" was an ideal lived out in San Francisco's Haight-Ashbury district, and later, with increased fervor, in the San Francisco Castro Street gay movement: sex anytime, anyplace and in any way one liked, aggressively indifferent to others' opinions.

Right now free love is in shadow, but Rousseau's myth makes itself felt in the pop-psychological realm. "It was your loving parents," writes Irene Kassorla, "anxious and guilt-ridden about their own sensuality, who unwittingly suppressed your instinctive erotic behaviors. . . . Parents teach, pressure and punish their impressionable children until most signs of sexual life are dead." A great deal is made of the natural masturbation of infants, which parents "kill." Were it not for parental stigmatizing, we would be naturally orgasmic, and thus content in all we do. Rousseau's noble savage is reincarnated as a guiltless, sensuous child.

This vision of reality does not stand much scrutiny. At least, it is a vision of reality unrelated to any known human experience. Plato was one of the first to note that society inevitably channels our desires away from certain possibilities: notably, from incest. (So far, only the furthest fringe advocates overthrowing incest taboos, though with the advent of birth control there is no "practical" reason why they ought to be respected.) Historian Lawrence Stone, surveying the history of sexuality in the West, writes, "Over the long history of Western civilization, there has been no such thing as 'normal sexuality.' Sexuality is a cultural artifact. . . ." That is, sexuality exists only as a socialized, cultural phenomenon; there is no noble savage.

Freedom to play

Perhaps more important, freedom is not necessarily diminished by social controls. It depends on what you mean by freedom. If freedom is the absence of controls, then of course controls destroy it. But if you think of freedom as something more like creativity or playfulness, then it certainly is not diminished by social controls. Andrew Greeley makes this point very eloquently. "My friend was deeply committed to her own marriage, and while she and her husband would not define themselves exactly as Christians, she was still willing to admit that the Christian ideal of marriage and the Christian concept of the relationship between sex and love were compelling. If sex were linked with love, then, she conceded, the result was almost inevitably something that looked like marriage. But sex didn't have to be linked with love; it could also be play, and play was casual, spontaneous, freewheeling, open-ended."

Greeley responded at the time by saying that sex was a serious business, and play was inevitably shallow. He later realized this was an inadequate response. In sexuality, play *is* important. But it doesn't follow that you play best with just anybody.

"A couple of months ago I encountered a 'with-it' marriage counselor (of vague Catholic antecedents) who repeated the argument.... This time I was ready.

" 'Do your children [both under ten] like to play?' I asked.

" 'Well of course they do.'

" 'And do they play with strangers, casual acquaintances, people they don't care about?'

" 'That's different,' she said, somewhat lamely."

Greeley's point is that you are freest with those you know well, whom you love, and with whom you are entirely comfortable. One might add that play almost always occurs within "the rules of the game." Children, the masters of play, take great interest in the rules and insist that everyone observe them.

Parental "repression" need not necessarily be killing children's spontaneous sexuality. It may be teaching children the rules of the game, enabling them to express their sexuality in a way that suits the community of people they live with and will be joined to through their sexuality.

Christian freedom

Christians have a very strong, fundamental commitment to freedom. Scripture teaches us that God's fundamental purposes are related to freedom: "It is for freedom that Christ set you free," in Paul's magnificent redundancy (Gal. 5:1). But what is freedom?

The biblical idea of freedom is first and foremost the freedom from oppressive powers. Yahweh, through Moses, freed Israel from Pharaoh's oppression. Through David God freed Israel from Philistine domination. God through Jesus freed all people from Satan's oppression. Freedom is never scripturally defined in some abstract condition; it is described as the absence of particular oppressions on particular people at particular times and places.

Freedom is also defined positively. God frees from oppressive powers in order that his people might spontaneously and passionately take up a loving relationship to him.

This idea of freedom can be transposed to the human level. What powers oppress us, keeping us from love? What loving relationships are offered to us?

Christians claim that loving relationships come within the bounds of marriage or celibacy. How can these be considered freedom, when they have so many restrictions? They can because they represent freedom from oppressive powers: principally, the oppression of individualism and selfishness.

Bruno Bettelheim writes, "The greatest happiness in marriage can come about only when true independence as socially equal human beings is enriched and made continually fascinating and satisfying for both partners by their being sexually completely secure with each other." Without that confident security, who can really make himself vulnerable, abandoning himself into love with another person?

Marriage also promises freedom from the oppression of sexual competitiveness. Few things so quickly destroy the joy of a relationship as the atmosphere of comparison. When a woman is compared to her neighbor, to a former or future lover, to a film star, she stops being a lover. She is a performer, a competitor. Everything is serious. Everything must be evaluated: How well did I do? When a man feels that he is in competition with other men, with other women, with fantasy figures, how can he let down and laugh, or cry? Marriage puts two people together for a lifetime and says to them: You are free to make of this anything you want. No one, nothing, will interfere.

Celibacy represents a different kind of freedom. It is freedom from depersonalized, uncommitted sex, but freedom for a very different kind of intimacy. The freedom is to the love of God, and the love of his people in his church. All Christians experience these, but the single person is free to give himself to them in a singular degree.

The freedom that Dr. Ruth supports—the freedom to like or dislike sex with peanut butter—is superficial, and in practice it often enslaves. It does not deal with the practical realities of who and what is enslaving a person, and toward what kind of love freedom should lead. In practice, it can enslave the individual to whims, to selfishness, and through these to isolation. The person who breaks off a relationship because of peanut butter often ends up with peanut butter as his only lasting companion. A biblical understanding of freedom is far more fruitful.

The couple were young professionals: he a reporter on the newspaper, she a lawyer. They were enthusiastic, friendly, excited about the church and their discovery of faith in Christ. It was during the orientation

*classes for church membership that their status came out. They were
not married. They were living together.*

*The pastor said nothing during the class, but the next morning called
Dominick, the reporter, to arrange a meeting. Dominick asked him
what it was about. The pastor said that he was concerned about the fact
that they were living together; the church believed strongly that a
foundation of commitment was essential for a loving sexual relationship. He would like to explore with them what commitment meant in
their relationship.*

*Dominick said, "Frankly, I don't see that it's any of your business."
He hung up, and the couple were never seen in church again.*

The fourth pathway out of our problems, to sexual salvation, is
privacy. Despite the widespread media exposure of sex, many people consider their own sexuality a private matter; they think that the
best way to protect it from oppressive forces is simply to keep it
shielded. This principle can be extended in many directions. It is the
argument for abortion rights. The point is not that abortion is
necessarily right; the point is that it is nobody's business but the
mother's. Similarly, the couple who refuse to discuss their relationship with the pastor simply assert that their sexual behavior is none
of their church's business.

Conservatives, too, are interested in privacy. The argument conservatives make against public-school sex education is sometimes a
privacy argument—that regardless of what is taught, it infringes on
the privacy of the family. The argument against pornography asserts the individual's right not to have his private thoughts invaded
by images he considers immoral or salacious. No conservative
wants the government invading the privacy of his home.

Yet sexual privacy must have some limits, for sexual acts have an
impact beyond the home. Sexual liaisons transmit deadly diseases,
affect the stability of family life, create babies. Private sexual habits
support a public pornography industry. No one argues that privacy
guarantees the right to abuse your children sexually, or even your
animals. How, though, are limits on privacy to be assessed?

The confessional
In the Catholic church, confession of sins to a priest was required for
every Christian by the seventeenth century. It was not up to the

individual to decide what topics were relevant to confession. By asking questions, the priest was to unmask sin in the individual. Some of the manuals gave the priest remarkable authority. "Tell everything," one manual instructed the priest to say. "Not only consummated acts, but sensual touchings, all impure gazes, all obscene remarks . . . all consenting thoughts." A confessing Christian could be asked about how often he had intercourse with his wife, in what positions, with what thoughts. It was truly an odd scene: the celibate priest delving into such matters in such detail.

Is it different from the scene in the psychiatrist's office? A client is encouraged to tell not merely what he has done, but the thoughts and feelings that accompanied them. For many psychoanalysts, sexual acts and feelings are laden with meaning. As with the priest, the psychiatrist only hears; he does not tell about himself. As with the priest, the psychiatrist seeks to help the individual come to terms with himself. Both priest and psychiatrist see themselves as kinds of physicians.

Are they? Sometimes yes, sometimes no. If they can really be healing physicians, then privacy can be relinquished. But what if they cannot really help, and what if they do not really care for the person they strip naked?

Consider a third setting: the Communist party. The individual's inmost thoughts must sometimes be known and corrected by the party. William Hinton's *Fanshen: A Documentary of Revolution in a Chinese Village* describes in incredible detail the self-criticisms that engaged Chinese peasants for days on end, long into the night, month after month and year after year, in small villages swallowed up by the Communist revolution. Nothing was irrelevant; not the smallest, most fleeting thought could be left out. One reads with a sense of wonder that a political movement could attract such faith.

These three contexts suggest, I think, what privacy is all about. It is about protection from the arrogance of human beings who, wanting to do good, and sometimes actually doing good, assume the rights of God over others. Human beings need protection from those who would control even the tiniest aspect of their lives—even their thoughts.

God, we know, has access to all our thoughts; there is no right of privacy from him. He is God, and he knows how to do his work so as to help, not harm, us. He does not destroy our freedom; he creates it. But no one else can usurp his role.

Why clothes?

God recognized the importance of privacy from the moment that sin came into the world. He made clothes for Adam and Eve, who, until they fell into sin, had been naked and unashamed. They had already made themselves fig-leaf loincloths, but God made garments from skin—clothes intended to last.

Why did they need clothes? They had the same bodies they had had from Creation, which God had called good. Yet they were ashamed, and covered their bodies. The problem was not with their bodies, but in what they and others might do with their bodies. They needed privacy for protection.

Anyone who has been mentally undressed by another—or has done the undressing—knows that shame is not in nakedness, but in the experience of being reduced to nothing more than a naked body. Clothing was needed to curb the tendency of sinful people to treat each other as mere objects of desire. Clothes keep our vulnerable sexuality under cover, until the conditions are right for us to disrobe—until we are protected by marriage from abuse.

How to treat shame

There is potential for confusion here, because sometimes the desire for privacy is produced by shame and sometimes by a motivation utterly different. For example, a person who doesn't want to go skinny dipping may be asked, "What are you ashamed of?" Quite possibly he is not ashamed of anything; he may honor his body by keeping it private. Shame, unlike that, is rooted in a negative self-image. The emotions of shame come from experiences in which we become ashamed of ourselves because we are unable to live effective lives. Shame is objective first, then subjective. For instance, a child may grow up ashamed of his body through experiences in which someone humiliates him because of his body.

Occasionally people try to eradicate shame by doing away with privacy. It doesn't work. To talk candidly about sex, to take off our clothes, to become "desensitized" by pornography, to try every possible sexual act, will not make us any less ashamed—only less sensitive. Such methods of attacking shame may really increase our shame, insofar as they increase our vulnerability to a pitiless world.

What may decrease shame—objective shame first, then subjective shame—are experiences that make our sexuality truly productive, loving and happy. When Paul wrote to the Romans, "I am not ashamed of the gospel," he did not mean primarily that he felt good about his message, but that the gospel was objectively effective. It would not let him down, "For it is the power of God for salvation to everyone who believes" (Rom. 1:16). To decrease sexual shame we need a style of life that will not let us down. Privacy is needed—privacy that shields our vulnerability, our nakedness, from those who do not love us and are not committed to our welfare.

The Communist party should not be allowed to penetrate a person's thoughts because it does not love, and it is not committed to any person's welfare. Its concern is always with the party, not people. The church and the psychiatrist may fail on the same score. For instance, the pastor who wishes to counsel Dominick on his living-together relationship: Is it the pastor's business to invade Dominick's privacy? Or is the pastor assuming the prerogatives of God? The answer depends on the degree to which the pastor, and the body of Christians he represents, deeply and effectively will commit themselves to Dominick's welfare. If the pastor's concern is merely to keep the church's rules, Dominick may have been right to hang up. But if the pastor could help Dominick escape from a shame-making cycle of uncommitted sexuality, then Dominick may have lost the chance of his life.

Sexual privacy is valuable, but not always. It can protect vulnerable human beings, but it can also isolate them from a healing community. Privacy can be an excuse for unlimited individualism.

How can you tell? You can only evaluate privacy by considering the particulars: who is being protected from whom, and for what purpose? Biblical wisdom is needed.

True salvation

We have looked at four ways in which the sexual revolution promises to overcome the fallenness of our sexuality: by creating equality between men and women, by educating in the "facts of life," by creating and encouraging sexual freedom, by insisting on personal privacy.

Christians, as we have seen, are interested in all these pathways. We believe deeply in equality, in education, in freedom, in privacy. But we have a distinctive understanding of each of these—an understanding that enhances and deepens the realism with which each of these ideals can be applied.

Nevertheless, at another point we balk completely. That is the idea that sexuality can be really redeemed without God. All ways out of sin depend on him, in some sense. Equality must be based on God's equal concern. Education at its best must include the wisdom that comes from God. Freedom is found in love, and God is love. Privacy is best understood not as a "no trespassing" sign on each individual's sexuality, but as a way of protecting vulnerable people made in God's image.

Christians often interact with the sexual revolution on its own level—as a practical contest as to whether Christians or secularists offer the most pleasure, the least pain, the best eroticism, the least destruction of families and persons. Christians may win such a contest. But in doing so we may lose the real struggle, which is to bring all things into proper relation with Christ. If we discuss sex only at a "practical" level, we have failed at our great calling: to proclaim the kingdom of God, to show his lordship over all—including sex and sexuality.

Chapter 10

OUR MINISTRY

Dan Simka returned home from a night meeting with one of his elders. The house was dark; Dan's wife was at a Bible study. Dan did not turn on any lights. He sat down on the sofa and wondered just what his ministry was accomplishing. In his hand he had the elder's scribbled letter of resignation.

The previous month, another elder had resigned, leaving a letter on Dan's desk. In it the elder had said he was separating from his wife; he did not feel fit to serve as a church leader any longer. Since then he had not been in church, nor had he returned Dan's calls. Dan had spent many hours with that couple, trying to help them. For nothing?

Now Tom. Tom was the sort of lay leader a pastor must have: reliable, unflappable. But last week Dan had discovered that Tom had been conducting an affair with a Sunday school teacher. Tom was repentant, but Dan had insisted that he needed a period out of leadership. In a small church with only five elders, they had lost two in one month.

Dan had prided himself on teaching candidly about sex. He had often preached about problems in marriage, pulling no punches in discussing adultery and premarital sex. Yet he never knew how people really reacted. They thanked him, nervously, for addressing the topic, but they *didn't let him know what they were thinking.*

Dan had always imagined the church as an alternative society, calling people to a different allegiance, and providing a wonderful shelter from the godless immorality of our age. Now he saw a different possibility—that of a church trumpeting a worn-out message about sex that few, inside or outside the church, really believed or felt able to live.

In an era of sexual confusion, Christians may be pardoned for taking an aggressive position on sexual morality. We think we know what is right, and we think the world is going to hell and would like to drag us with it. Why should we acquiesce to pornography's pollution? Why shrug our shoulders over promiscuity, as though it really were a purely private matter? We know how important sex is. We understand how God wants us to use it. We know that his instructions are for our good, and for anyone's good. We would be very much to blame if we failed to include sex and sexuality within our ministry to the world around us.

Yet our sexual ministry does not begin with the world around us. Our ministry must begin with ourselves. After all, Christians are not simply proclaiming a message. We are issuing an invitation. We invite "the world" to leave its worldliness and join the community of worship and witness called the church. The church is the place where salvation, including sexual salvation, must begin. We cannot be very convincing in proclaiming sexual salvation to the world if we are not experiencing it in the church.

Both the Old and New Testaments teach about sex with the redeemed community, not pagan society, in view. Paul's letters show he was not principally concerned that Christians critique their neighbors' sexual habits. (There was plenty to critique in Greco-Roman sexual practices, but he hardly raises the issue.) He was chiefly concerned that Christians' lives reflect the glory of the gospel. Thus Paul's ultimate, exasperated plea to the Corinthians can only be addressed to believers: "Do you not know that your body is a temple of the Holy Spirit, who is in you, whom you have received from God? You are not your own; you were bought at a price. Therefore honor God with your body" (1 Cor. 6:19–20).

Paul wanted the church to be a counterculture, showing itself distinct from its surroundings. He expected Christians to strengthen and encourage one another, so that they could together reflect the ultimate counterculture, the kingdom of God.

Sexual ministry: What we are doing

In the past twenty years American Christians have launched a significant sexual ministry within the church. Occasional sermons have treated sex with a frankness that would have been unthinkable a generation earlier. Special seminars on sex—particularly for young people, but sometimes for married couples—have proliferated. Counseling ministries have grown up, and they deal increasingly with sexual problems. Some Christian counselors have even specialized in sexual therapy.

Ministries have been created to deal with specialized issues of sexuality. A few ministries scattered around the country have attempted to minister to the problems of homosexuals. Numerous ministries, often linked to churches, try to strengthen marriages through seminars and retreats. (One of the more popular manifestations being the marriage encounter weekend.) Others encourage single people. You could attend many churches for years without hearing a word about sex, but on the other hand, people looking for help in their sexual lives can find it, if they are willing to look.

In addition, a good number of Christian books have dealt with sexuality, on every level from serious theology to "how to." The topic of sex does not lack for a full and candid discussion by Christians in print.

Yet the most potent force in sexual ministry remains the most "old-fashioned"—the gospel of grace. In our world's view, each individual is lord of his life, trying to order his universe (and his sexual experiences) to please himself. The gospel utterly transforms such a view. In Christ, each individual submits to Christ's lordship; he sees that the universe was made to please Christ. A Christian must, because of the gospel, view others as equal to him in the eyes of God. Further, he understands that instead of others' existing to meet his needs, he is called to serve their needs. On this basis, enduring and just relationships can be made.

As long as people in the church act on the same premises as those outside the church, searching for personal happiness at all costs, seminars on sexual technique or on communication in marriage will not stop the parade of divorces and adulteries and sexual experiments. All these are attempts individuals make to find happiness, and they will continue the attempts until they are convinced that Jesus spoke the truth in saying that a person must lose his life to find it. The most important sexual ministry remains preaching the gospel.

Within that context, three areas of ministry particularly need attention in the church: teaching our children about sex, strengthening our marriages, and developing a sense of purpose for single people.

Sex education
Every living community must pass on its beliefs to the next generation. Therefore, Christians must teach their children in the faith what sex is all about. Unfortunately, practically all that we have accomplished so far in this regard is a pervasive negativism toward secular sex education.

Most school systems offer some sex education, and while its effectiveness is not observable to the casual eye, reformers urge a more comprehensive curriculum, beginning at an earlier age, and even incorporating school-based clinics that would offer contraceptives to sexually active teenagers. Many Christians have their doubts about this kind of education. Can you really teach about sex without teaching values? Furthermore, is a public classroom the very best place to learn about sex? Doesn't teaching it there remove sex from the family context where it belongs, making it a part of the impersonal public sector? Can the meaning of sex and the meaning of trigonometry really be conveyed in the same manner?

Those who favor increased public school sex education usually concede that parents and churches could do a better job. Yet, as we noted earlier, they make a devastating counterpoint: parents and churches are not doing a better job. They are often not doing anything. Many young people get their sex education through pornography. Parents are often intimidated by the task. Some parents can only pass on their own misinformation. Few churches offer a comprehensive sex-education program. In view of this situation, Christians who "just say no"—no to every proposal for public-school sex education—look suspiciously like people who prefer their children to remain ignorant.

Churches must help parents teach about sex. If we leave sex education strictly to parents, we know that many will fail to provide it. And what about young Christians whose parents are not believers? If the church doesn't approve of the sex education they get from society, the church has a responsibility to teach them. When churches help parents teach children about sex in an organized, comprehensive manner, no parents will be able to say, "We just never got around to it," or, "I didn't know what to say." And none of our children will grow up claiming that "No one ever talked to me about sex."

What keeps parents from organizing one or two Saturdays a year at church to gather with their children in the various age groups to talk together about the "facts of life" and what they mean to Christians? My suspicion is that if we organized such education, some of our non-Christian neighbors would become interested in joining us.

The content of Christian sex education

Ethicist Stanley Hauerwas insists that ethical behavior is not brought about by drawing up lists of right and wrong actions. Ethical behavior is created by ethical people—by people of character. Christian sex education ought to try not merely to tell the truth about sex, but to form people who want to live up to the truth. There is a vast difference between teaching morals and training in godliness.

That is one reason why sexual values need to be taught within the family. There, sex cannot be an impersonal, abstract subject. It is taught by the person who has, by practicing it, brought a family into being. The "teacher" is looking at a "student" who owes his existence to the teacher's practice of sex. That makes the subject inescapably personal.

Children observe just how well their parents practice their sexuality. Any father who demonstrates love and respect for his wife, for example, is likely to raise children who appreciate loving and respectful marriages. They have seen it. They understand what it requires. And they will, if they admire their parents' marriage, be open even to the rules their parents insist are necessary. As Andrew Greeley writes, "If it is clear that the parents have obtained great enjoyment and satisfaction from their own sexual relationship, the children are perfectly willing and indeed eager to find out what their values are—how they have managed it when so many others have failed."

Sex education ought to center on parents, but the church as a whole needs to participate. For one thing, few Christian parents show all the Christian virtues. Ask their kids. (Paul Pearsall reports that more than half of the men and women in his sample had negative memories of the way their parents interacted. I doubt this is true only of non-Christian families.)

And not all styles of healthy sexuality can be modeled by any one family: Single-parent families cannot model marriage, while intact marriages cannot model a healthy single life. Children need surrogate parents—"mothers" and "fathers," "aunts" and "uncles" from the family of faith to show them the many positive possibilities of sexuality. They can find such people in the church.

Besides that, young people need one another's support if they are going to live a different kind of life. Most church youth groups try (with varying success) to develop an environment of peer support and accountability, an atmosphere of worship and service, and a sense of participation in the larger body of Christ. But most groups of my acquaintance keep the content mainly "spiritual." If they talk about sex at all, they do it briefly, and they do it for kids who are old enough to know all the biological facts of life already. Why such a slight, late effort, when we all know the serious implications of sex for young people?

A group of Christian young people who love one another, who are willing to take responsibility for one another's integrity, and who want to serve and worship God together, can learn about sex in a distinctively Christian way. They can support one another in a Christian lifestyle. They can protect one another from sexual predators. Adolescents and preteens are enormously affected by their peers, both for good and for evil. Christian sex education ought to foster positive peer influence. It should help young people realize their responsibility for one another within the family of faith.

Teaching right and wrong

Ethical people are not formed by hectic warnings from elders who see danger on every side—elders who mainly seem frightened. Neither are they formed by long, inconclusive dialogues in which nothing vital seems to be at stake.

Ethical people are almost inevitably those who have grown up with absolutes administered in love, and have grappled to understand for themselves what these absolutes mean and do not mean.

Absolutes—the plain declaration of right and wrong—can certainly become oppressive, mechanical, and pharisaical. In the wrong hands, they nearly always do. But absolutes also can, in the right loving hands, show that virtue is not a mere sentiment; virtue demonstrates itself in action. Absolutes express the conviction that evil is an active, even tangible, threat to our well-being. People who have grappled with absolutes are not saved by absolutes. Rather, they come to the limits of themselves and of the absolutes. But in doing so, they achieve a clear understanding that good and evil are decided every day in the actions of the body, that evil cannot be erased by an apology, and that good cannot be done by merely wishing it done. Our lives are at stake every day. Those who know this become people of character.

In the realm of sexuality, our age offers virtually no absolutes—or even workable guidance. ("Don't hurt anybody" usually works out to be mere sentiment.) For instance, Dr. Ruth seems to know the answer to every question, but she does not have any advice whatsoever for the most critical question for young people: When it is appropriate to begin having sex. "When is the right time to start having sex, to have it for the first time? I am asked that question again and again. . . . I always tell them, 'Don't do it until you are sure you want to do it.' That always seems to be just what they want to hear."

So much for guidance!

Christians can tell young people when it is right to have sex for the first time: on the day you marry. We should tell them this with firmness and conviction.

We need also to give much more specific guidance about dating. Perhaps there are no absolutes, but there is certainly clearer guidance than most teenagers get. What is the aim of dating? What kinds of physical expressions, from kissing to petting, are valuable? When are they valuable? As things are today, many teenagers start out convinced that they would like to wait for marriage to have sex. However, within the highly private environment of dating, they soon drift into touching each other—into foreplay. The body being what it is, foreplay leads to sex. Or, if it does not, a kind of iron discipline is required to stop short of sex. We are in need of a radical review of dating practices.

As any parent knows, however, this is all but impossible for parents to do alone. Teenagers cannot be controlled. Unless there is peer support in setting a different style of dating, it will never be done. A body of young believers who care about one another will have to establish its own counterculture. With the help and encouragement of their parents, they will have to make their own standards.

Strengthening marriages

In contrast to our weak attempts to teach our children, Christians have worked to strengthen marriages. Marriage enrichment retreats and courses, barely heard of twenty years ago, have become common. Professional counseling is widely available for marriages with problems.

Yet we must do a great deal more to face the requirements of marriage in today's climate. I see this most dramatically in our almost complete silence about adultery.

Adultery is undoubtedly the most potent destroyer of marriages. Yet we talk easily about less potent problems—communication, for example—and ignore this one. Studies indicate that adultery is extremely widespread within the church. Philip Blumstein and Pepper Schwartz, in their study of American couples, reported that "Those who attend church or synagogue regularly are much more conservative when it comes to what they believe about sex. They feel that sex and love are inseparable, they oppose 'pornography,' and when they are heterosexual, they do not favor equal rights for homosexuals. But at the same time, there is very little difference between religious and nonreligious people when it comes to how they act. They have the same amount of sex. They are just as satisfied. They have no more and no less conflict about sex. And they are just as traditional about the woman's right to initiate it.

"But perhaps the most startling finding is that religious people are as non-monogamous as anyone else. However attached people may be to religious institutions, they do not seem to be insulated from the temptations of the flesh."

A *Christianity Today* survey of subscribers found that 23 percent of respondents admitted to extramarital intercourse. (This is in line with Blumstein and Schwartz's findings.) A parallel survey of pastors found that 12 percent had committed adultery while in local church ministry.

Almost one quarter of the married people sitting in the pews of the average church have committed adultery—not last week, of course, but at some time in their married lives. It seems reasonable to assume that, for the 23 percent, adultery was among the most momentous events of their lives. They may often think of it, even in church. And yet those acts are clothed in total silence. How then can they be forgiven? God does, of course, forgive; but how does the sinner receive that forgiveness in fullness when there is no word of forgiveness given by his church?

At the same time, the very real virtue of the three-quarters who have been faithful goes unrecognized—for nothing is said of them, either. Whatever has enabled their marriages to remain pure remains a mystery to those who need it most.

In this silence, the occasional act of church discipline—such as is inspired by the well-publicized failure of a pastor—will seem extreme to many church members. One-quarter of the average congregation, and one-eighth of the pastors, has done the same thing. One unfortunate individual gets caught and punished. The church is unpracticed in discipline and in forgiveness. People respond awkwardly, and sometimes meanly. Discipline often seems to miss its goal of repentance, forgiveness, and restoration.

It is probably impossible to hope that in the near future we could develop a different atmosphere of accountability for the whole church. But at least we could look for ways to develop it in particular groups within the church—among the church leadership, for example.

We can also address the issue publicly. I am not suggesting that cases of adultery be publicized. But I am suggesting that at least pastors preach about this sin (as they have not in my generation), that teaching about repentance, forgiveness, and restoration be presented regularly in every congregation, and that counseling and encouragement for troubled marriages be offered more aggressively. Silence serves no one. Adultery and other deep marital troubles are quite common in our churches. How can a realistic sexual salvation begin to operate until the reality of our troubles is uncovered and dealt with frankly and compassionately?

Singles ministry

In recent times, Christians have been most successful at portraying the desirability of life-long, loving marriage. Of course, this success cannot be taken for granted; just ten years ago traditional monogamy seemed to be in trouble. Today, however, most people have lost interest in "alternative" marriages. Even childbearing has regained some of its traditional prominence.

But what about those who are unmarried? Among them, traditional Christian ethics have been almost entirely overwhelmed. Only a fraction of those who marry in America are virgins. "Living together" has become mundane; and sexual intercourse has become extremely common—the norm, in fact—in serious relationships between single adults.

For the most part, these single people are not "swingers" or "sexual gourmets." They want what everyone else wants: not to be alone. To many of them, sexual intimacy seems to be a fundamental human need. It certainly is a fundamental pleasure. Yet they are not married, and some never will be. Some are divorced. Some are widowed. Some are homosexuals.

Church singles groups have exploded in the last decade, trying to meet the needs of these people. There is a plainly sexual dimension: people attend because they meet people of their own age and situation. They hope to find companions, possibly a mate. Pastors sometimes denigrate the "meet and be met" function of these singles groups, but it is an important purpose. Paul himself thought celibacy was an undesirable state for some: "If they cannot control themselves, they should marry, for it is better to marry than to burn with passion" (1 Cor. 7:9). Christians have a stake in removing barriers to marriage so that people are free to take this advice.

Yet singles groups suffer when they become exclusively a launching pad for escape from singleness. Sometimes they seem to underline a non-Christian message: that genital sex is the end-all and be-all of life. Thus single people meet in the church instead of the singles bar, but with the same ultimate purpose—to escape from the hell of celibacy.

This might be less troubling if we could guarantee that every single person could marry. But that is not the case in our society. Some have no interest in marriage. Others foresee no possibility of marriage. Still others, mangled by an abusive marriage and divorce, cannot imagine wanting to try marriage again.

Kenneth Kantzer points out the disproportionate number of young women in Christian congregations. Many of these will not marry if they insist on marrying Christians. Kantzer says, "To me

it's terribly important that an unmarried woman is not an incomplete person. She can be complete without a full expression of certain sexual aspects of herself because the essential part of her is her likeness to God."

Many people, however—including Christians—find it hard to imagine real completeness without genital sexuality. Celibacy seems like a prison sentence. We have practically written this biblical gift out of the church. Must we always be embarrassed to recommend the pattern of life that our Lord, the apostle Paul, and nearly all of the church fathers followed? Surely Paul's words to the Corinthians suggest something better. Surely our singles groups need to apply themselves to the task of again seeing celibacy as a gift of the Holy Spirit to the church, as a positive witness to the world, whether for a short period or for an entire lifetime.

The early centuries of monasticism may help us. Christians who tried celibacy in isolation discovered that they needed the structure of communal life. They developed systems of spiritual guidance, of corporate worship, of shared resources, of responsibility to the group. Perhaps singles groups need to become far more disciplined and directed. Nobody can doubt that a single Christian who wants to live a celibate life is going against our culture. He or she needs the strength and encouragement—and the structure—of a group that has different intentions.

What is more, the church needs such groups. If celibacy is truly a gift, we should expect single people to put it to work in God's work. They have something unique to offer the body of Christ. If we looked to them for singular service and leadership, we might transform the victim mentality that many singles fall into.

Our outward ministry

Suppose that we manage these reforms. Suppose we organize sex education for our children through the church, end the silence about sexual temptation and failure, and establish singles groups that demonstrate the giftedness of celibacy. What then would be our ministry to the world outside?

It is obvious that our prime ministry to the world outside would already be in operation: We would be a living witness to a different kingdom. We would show by our lives as well as our words that there is an alternative to the sexuality of our day. We would be able to invite people into the church in such a way that the invitation was an invitation to holiness.

Our chief responsibility is to be what God has called us to be, and to tell the good news of Jesus to anyone who will listen. We are not really called to preach our sexual ethics; we are called to live them. What we preach is, above all, forgiveness and the possibility of a new life.

We do have other duties, however. While we live primarily as citizens of God's kingdom, we remain citizens of earthly societies. We owe allegiance (though a decidedly lesser allegiance) to these societies too. We have something to offer them—something that is distinctively ours as Christians.

America is not going to become the kingdom of God, and even if its sexual ethics became conservative and "Christian," they would not be truly Christian. As Walther Eichrodt wrote, the same thing done by different people is not the same thing. Our ethics, lived without the grace of God and the life of the Holy Spirit, are merely the law. We need to be quite clear about this. The scriptural law is good, coming from God. But we are not particularly called to preach the law to our society.

What besides preaching are we called to do? We are called to care for the weak and to stand up for them. In the words of Proverbs, we must "speak for the dumb" and "defend the rights of the poor and needy" (31:8–9). Who are the poor and the needy in today's sexual realm? Who gets run over by our steam-rollering society? It is the young—particularly young, pregnant women. It is divorced women, cast aside as worthless. It is the physically unattractive. It is those with homosexual desires.

All these are likely to end up sexually unwanted. They do not qualify for Playboy eroticism, nor for marital domesticity. The best our age offers them is the possibility of an occasional fling, since anything goes.

Often Christians take a stand on public issues in terms of preserving our own rights. We speak for the supposedly "moral majority." We might be more effective—and we would certainly be closer to the prophetic tradition—if we spoke up for the interests of those, unlike ourselves, who have no voice. On abortion, the most powerful word we speak is on behalf of those who cannot speak—the children who die before they are born. There are other casualties of the sexual revolution, including casualties who are willing participants in their own destruction. They do not always know what they are doing to themselves. If we know, we need to care enough to tell them—and to fight for them.

In so doing, we are not exactly fighting for their sexual salvation. That can come only through Christ, and within the context of his salvation of their entire lives. We are fighting to protect our society from its tendency toward evil and abuse of persons.

In Jesus' kingdom, and in it alone, people will find full sexual salvation. Whatever salvation we experience here and now is fragmentary, broken. It is only a beginning—though it is a beginning that will go on forever.

We are being saved, and our message is ultimately one of idealism and hope. This is what we believe, live, and proclaim. We must not get bogged down in moralisms and condemnations. Christians believe unashamedly in absolutes, but they cannot be detached from our absolute hope in the salvation of Christ. Our sexuality is one part of a wonderful work that God is doing.

BIBLIOGRAPHY

OF SIGNIFICANT WORKS

Love: Christian Romance, Marriage, Friendship, by Diogenes Allen (Cambridge, MA: Cowley Publications, 1987). A thoughtful philosophical study, not technical, of different kinds of love.

God and Marriage, by Geoffrey W. Bromiley (Grand Rapids, MI: Eerdmans, 1980). A brief, serious, conservative look at virtually all the relevant biblical texts.

American Couples: Money, Work, Sex, by Philip Blumstein and Pepper Schwartz (New York: William Morrow, 1983). An exhaustive sociological study.

Between the Sexes: Foundations for a Christian Ethic of Sexuality, by Lisa Sowle Cahill (Philadelphia: Fortress, 1985). This book takes a rather scattered scholarly approach, but offers some excellent insights.

Sex and the American Teenager, by Robert Coles and Geoffrey Stokes (New York: Harper & Row, 1985). A sociological study.

The History of Sexuality, Volume I: An Introduction, by Michel Foucault, tr. Robert Hurley (New York: Random House, 1978). A highly influential book, which makes the claim that the sexual revolution is not a reversal of Victorianism, but a continuation. Not light reading.

The Use of Pleasure: The History of Sexuality, Volume 2, by Michel Foucault, tr. Robert Hurley (New York: Random House, 1985). An analysis of the classical Greek heritage in regard to sexuality.

The Care of the Self: The History of Sexuality, Volume 3, by Michel Foucault, tr. Robert Hurley (New York: Pantheon, 1986). An analysis of Greco-Roman sexuality, in the period leading up to the Christian era.

Innocent Ecstasy: How Christianity Gave America an Ethic of Sexual Pleasure, by Peter Gardella (New York: Oxford University Press), 1985. An entertaining and informative history of sex and Christianity in America.

Men and Marriage, by George Gilder (New York: Pelican, 1986). A much-hated book (originally published in 1973 as *Sexual Suicide*), original and thought provoking. Some conservative Christians love Gilder because he is in favor of the traditional family, and against feminism—but they shouldn't. Approaching the relationship of male and female as an evolutionary adaptation, as Gilder does, yields a sub-Christian idea of family. Still, there is lots to learn here.

Sexual Intimacy: Love and Play, by Andrew M. Greeley (New York: Warner, 1988). Greeley's idea of sexual fulfillment reminds me of thoughts I had in junior high school. Still, a number of good insights appear through the steam.

"Relations Natural and Unnatural: A Response to John Boswell's Exegesis of Romans 1," by Richard B. Hays, *The Journal of Religious Ethics* (Spring / 1986). A remarkably fine essay that ought to be required reading for any Christian who wants to talk about the ethics of homosexuality.

Rebonding, by Donald Joy (Waco, TX: Word, 1986). A very interesting popular book that (along with its predecessor, *Bonding*) reinterprets biblical sexual ethics in light of anthropological studies on bonding. Joy sometimes falls into an almost biomechanical understanding of love and marriage, but in mild doses this serves as a corrective to the spiritualized understanding often current today.

Embodiment: An Approach to Sexuality and Christian Theology, by James B. Nelson (Minneapolis, MN: Augsburg, 1979). Well written, thoughtful, but on the whole an example of how the spirit of the age can be packaged as Christian theology. A much-quoted book.

Sex in the World's Religions, by Geoffrey Parrinder (New York: Oxford University Press, 1980). An excellent survey of the great religions and their teachings about sex.

Sex for Christians, by Lewis Smedes (Grand Rapids, MI: Eerdmans, 1976). Fluent, realistic, and biblical. Smedes deals with the difficult ethical questions in a way that communicates to educated laypeople without sacrificing theological astuteness. There are some weak spots, especially in his section on petting, but this remains the best book available.

"Sex in the West," by Lawrence Stone, *The New Republic* (July 8, 1985). A good summary by an eminent historian of what we know about the history of sexuality in Europe and America.

OTHER WORKS CITED: BOOKS
Surviving and Other Essays, by Bruno Bettelheim (New York: Vintage Books), 1980.

The Rampant God, by Nigel Davies (New York: William Morrow, 1984).

Nice Girls Do, by Irene Kassorla (New York: Berkeley, 1982).

The Act of Marriage: The Beauty of Sexual Love, by Tim and Beverly LaHaye (Grand Rapids, MI: Zondervan, 1976).

Intimacy: The Essence of Male and Female, by Shirley Gehrke (San Rafael, CA: Luthman, Mehetabel & Co., 1972).

Super Marital Sex: Loving for Life, by Paul Pearsall (New York: Doubleday, 1987).

The Ethics of Sex, by Helmut Thielicke (New York: Harper & Row, 1964).

Dr. Ruth's Guide to Good Sex, by Dr. Ruth Westheimer (New York: Warner, 1983).

Eros Defiled: The Christian and Sexual Sin, by John White (Downers Grove, IL: InterVarsity, 1977).

American Teens Speak: Sex, Myths, TV, and Birth Control: The Planned Parenthood Poll (New York: Louis Harris and Associates, 1986.

OTHER WORKS CITED: MAGAZINES

"Everything Else You Always Wanted to Know About Sex," by Jared Diamond, *Discover*, April 1985.

"Why Men Fear Commitment," by Warren Farrell, *Glamour*, August 1986.

"Homosexuality, the Behavioral Sciences and the Church," by Stanton L. Jones. An unpublished address.

" 'I Need Space': Cracking the Intimacy Code," by Arlene Kagle, *Mademoiselle*, April 1988.

"Who Are the Happiest Couples," by Helen Singer Kaplan, *Redbook*, November 1986.

"Interview with James Nelson," *U.S. Catholic*, October 1986.

"Six Sex Mistakes Most Wives Make," by Alexandra Penney, *Ladies Home Journal*, March 1988.

"The News About Infidelity," by Maggie Scarf, *Cosmopolitan*, April 1987.

"Great Sex: Reclaiming a Christian Sexual Ethic," by Tim Stafford, *Christianity Today*, October 2, 1987.

"The Christian Mind and the Challenge of Gender Relations," by Mary Stewart Van Leeuwen, *The Reformed Journal*, September 1987.

"How Common Is Pastoral Indiscretion?" *Leadership Journal*, Winter 1988.

"Cosmo's Private Sex Survey," *Cosmopolitan*, July 1988.